D0178115

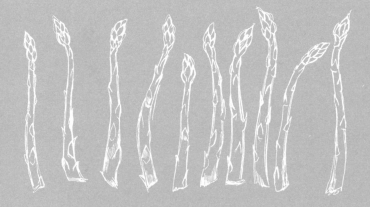

FRESH

FRESH

Simple, delicious recipes to make you feel energised!

DONAL SKEHAN

To Sofie, my beautiful bride, for shooting the cover photo
and for not shooting me!

contents

introduction

The world of food is changing. It's hard not to notice the huge increase in healthy recipes, including options for vegetarian, vegan and gluten-free diets and more. With a greater knowledge of food, ingredients and their origins it is hard for us to avoid the fact that what we put into our body affects so many aspects of our lifestyle. This is pushing us to make better food choices, but with the wealth of trendy new ingredients and cooking methods, it is essential that we don't lose a connection with our knowledge of cooking and food that really tastes good in our search for healthier options. For, as much as I want to eat well, I want to be excited by the food I make, and to still taste those essential layers of flavour that excite me as a cook.

Like so many of us, my lifestyle is busy and fast-paced, often making it tricky to prioritise eating food that is nutritious and energising. Over the last few years I found myself frustrated and exhausted with early starts and long working hours; I was working weekends, juggling different projects, travelling and most importantly, not having enough time to enjoy the food I was eating. As someone who works in food full-time, it felt like the most strange and disconnected problem, which didn't sit well with me. The catalyst for the change in my approach to both life and food came recently when I found myself in hospital while filming in Vietnam. Feeling dreadful and on my second round of antibiotics, I headed home to do a string of 20 dates for a live cooking tour in Ireland. I hit absolute exhaustion; I never knew I could be that tired and unwell. These issues became the inspiration to write a cookbook full of recipes that would combat these problems. Beyond the recipes, I took time to reflect on just how I was spending my time. I learned that while stress can be a positive in our lives, pushing us to achieve, periods of stress without any recovery time was what was really bringing me down. I stopped saying yes to work that wouldn't work for me, I prioritised spending time with friends and family and, most importantly, I made time to cook and eat the food that inspired and nourished me.

I now aim for balanced eating, which allows me to enjoy the food I've always loved but also puts a focus on including as much seasonal fresh fruit and vegetables, grains and smaller amounts of high-quality meat in my diet. I take my time to cook and I take my time to eat. These 'rules' allow me to stay true to what I believe good home cooking to be.

It can be difficult to maintain these ideals but one of the biggest changes you can make is to plan ahead. Spending time once a week shopping for ingredients or simply writing down what you plan to make can really increase your chances of making better food choices. When I make the time, I boil grains, wash salad leaves, prepare salad dressings, bake bread, mix up marinades, toast seeds and roast vegetables and store them for later. These are all small steps that will help me pull together a meal

very simply throughout the week. Shopping for ingredients plays a key part in the process and although I try to buy most produce as fresh as possible, I like to make sure I have those key meal-building ingredients stocked in my store cupboard. It then becomes so much easier to create a meal around them.

With all that in mind, the recipes in this book harness my love of simple, healthy home-cooked food. I've put fruit and vegetables at the forefront of most of them, explored spice and texture, layers of flavours and different cooking methods, all to achieve food which is nutritious while at its core being truly delicious. And yes, I have unashamedly used a few of those fashionable new ingredients and cooking methods, but only where I have tried and tested them and believe they are worth using.

The chapters are built around the way I like to eat. There are recipes for hearty and filling breakfasts that can be prepared in advance or cooked in a short space of time, giving options for nutritious morning eating. My world tends to require lunch on the go so I have written recipes to satisfy just this: filling lunchbox options which are substantial enough to keep you going while also being jam-packed full of fresh and healthy ingredients. I think for most people dinner can go one of two ways: simple nourishment thrown together with little effort in minutes or a meal where more time is allowed to savour the cooking process. Both these scenarios are covered with plenty of quick cook suppers and relaxed dinner recipes. With so many of us now having different dietary requirements, there are plenty of sweet dessert recipes that offer gluten-free, dairy-free and in some cases sugar-free options – but always with the emphasis on taste and flavour. Finally, in the store cupboard chapter you will find recipes that I believe are fundamental for lighter eating: spice mixes, healthy breads, roast vegetables and sauces, helping to give that perfect finishing touch to your dish.

At its heart, this is a book of healthy, fresh recipes that are as nourishing as they are delicious. I hope you enjoy both cooking and eating them!

the
best
meal
of the
day

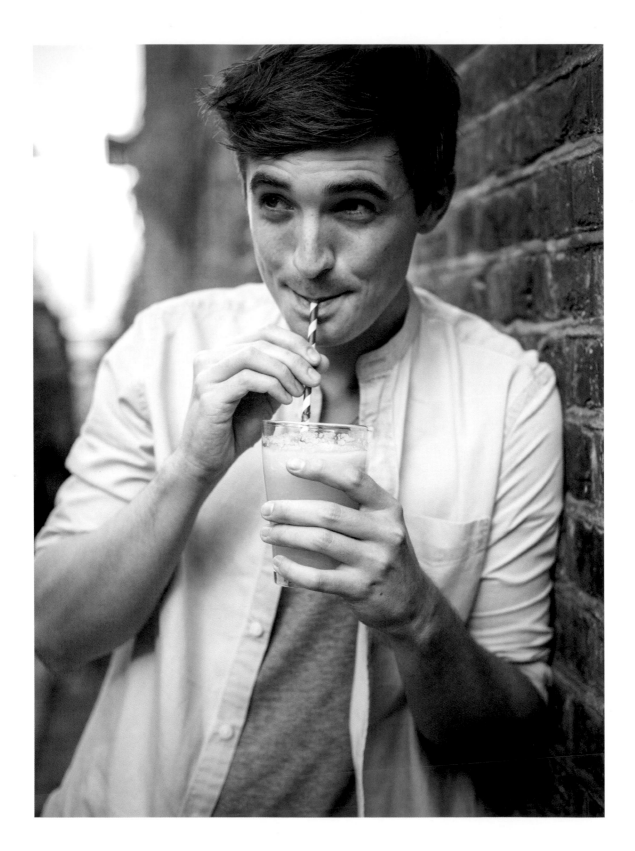

There is truth in the title: breakfast is the best meal of the day. It provides a great starting point for eating food that is full of healthy ingredients, that will fill you up and keep you going throughout the day. I used to struggle with everyday breakfasts and I put it largely down to not having a collection of recipes that excited me, either to make or to eat. Breaking away from the mindless treadmill of cereal and toast doesn't have to be that tricky.

Probably the most important place to start is to mix up what you eat in the morning as often as possible. Between juices, smoothies, porridge, granola, toast toppers, healthier pancakes and plenty of options with eggs, having a variety of breakfast options is key when it comes to breaking the cycle. I fear juicing and smoothies often fall into the category of faddy diet trends, but since I started, they have both gone out and come back into fashion, proving they are here to stay. Both provide an instant hit of nutrients with and without fibre, but please don't confuse one with the other. I've had more than a couple of queries about juice recipes that didn't quite work out and when I delved a little deeper, I discovered they had been chucked in a blender. Juices are to be made in a juicer and smoothies in a blender. There are plenty of ideas for both here but do try to include greens as much as possible when making them. I'm rather proud of the Juicer Muffins in this chapter as they use up all that leftover pulp from making juices, and are properly tasty too.

Poached Egg with Spinach, Sweet Potato Rösti and Healthy Hollandaise or Huevos Rancheros Scambled Eggs served on corn tortillas make for a generous Saturday breakfast, while Za'atar Quinoa Poached Eggs or Apple, Cinnamon and Pecan Porridge are great snappy everyday options. If you often find you don't have time in the morning, I hope these recipes will convince you to carve out an extra 30 minutes at the start of the day to eat well.

4 Ways Super Juices

Apple, Carrot and Ginger Juice

Serves 1
2 eating apples
2 carrots
3cm slice of fresh ginger
Ice cubes, to serve

1. Roughly slice or chop the apples, carrots and ginger so that they fit into your juicer's feeder tube and process until you have a frothy orange liquid.

2. Pour over ice to serve. If you want more heat from the ginger, double the quantity.

Super Cleansing Juice

Serves 1
2 eating apples
1 carrot
1 slice of lemon with rind
¼ yellow pepper, deseeded
5cm piece of cucumber
5cm piece of celery
5cm piece of broccoli stem
5cm piece of raw beetroot
Ice cubes, to serve

1. Roughly chop or slice the fruit and vegetables so that they fit into your juicer's feeder tube.

2. Process the juice until you have a vibrant purple juice. Serve immediately over ice.

Even if you have never tried a juice before, these combinations are bound to convince you that juices with vegetables can be absolutely delicious! Sweet, zingy and fresh with citrus or ginger, these are an incredibly healthy way to start the day.

Green Goblin Super Juice

Serves 1

2 green eating apples, halved if necessary
1 large handful of baby leaf spinach
1 small handful of kale
2.5cm slice of cucumber
1cm slice of lime with rind
Ice cubes, to serve

1. Place one of the apples in the feeder tube of your juicer and top with the spinach and kale leaves. Add the other apple to create a leafy green sandwich (this will allow you to get the maximum juice) and process.

2. Add the rest of the ingredients to the juicer and continue to juice. Pour the rich green liquid over a glass filled with ice.

Watermelon Zinger

Serves 1

½ watermelon, peeled and chopped
5cm piece of cucumber
1 red apple
1 slice of lime
1 small thumb-sized piece of fresh ginger
Ice cubes, to serve

1. Place all the ingredients into the feeder tube of your juicer and process them through.

2. Serve immediately in an ice filled glass.

I always feel guilty dumping the pulp from my juicer into the compost bin, which is why I thought the moist pulp would be the perfect addition to a breakfast muffin. A quick search online made me realise I wasn't the first genius to think that idea up. So here goes: these are what I deem THE BEST JUICER MUFFINS in the world – tried and tested by me, my family and my dog. We approve – let's hope you do too!

Juicer Muffins with Chocolate Glaze

1. Preheat the oven to 180°C (160°C fan) and line a 12-hole muffin tin with paper cases.

2. Mix all the dry ingredients together in a large mixing bowl and make a well in the centre. In a large measuring jug, whisk together the date syrup, milk, eggs, bananas, juicer pulp and coconut oil. Pour the wet ingredient mixture into the dry ingredients and fold through until just combined.

3. Divide the mixture between the individual muffin cases and bake for 25 minutes, or until they have risen and a skewer inserted in the centre comes out clean. Allow the muffins to cool completely on a wire rack while you prepare the glaze.

4. In a bowl, whisk together the cacao powder, honey and coconut oil until you have a smooth mixture. If the coconut oil is still warm allow the mix to cool slightly before glazing.

5. Spread each muffin with a heaped teaspoon of the glaze and sprinkle with sea salt, cocoa nibs or bee pollen. The muffins will keep for 5 days in an airtight container.

Makes 12 muffins

125g plain flour
75g wholemeal flour
200g rolled oats
3 tbsp sunflower seeds
1 tsp baking powder
1 tsp salt
75ml date syrup
250ml nut or soya milk
2 large eggs
2 bananas, mashed
150g juicer pulp
3 tbsp coconut oil, melted

For the chocolate glaze
3 tbsp raw cacao powder
2 tbsp honey
100g coconut oil, melted
Pinch of sea salt
2 tbsp raw cacao nibs or bee pollen, to decorate

Blueberry and Chia Seed Muffins

Muffins are perfect for a quick breakfast on the go. These blueberry and chia seed muffins are packed with healthy ingredients, which will keep you going on any busy morning. I normally make them the night before and grab one or two just before I leave the house.

Makes 12 muffins

125g plain flour
75g wholemeal flour
200g rolled oats
1 tsp baking powder
1 tsp ground cinnamon
3 tbsp chia seeds
1 tsp salt
75g brown sugar
2 bananas, mashed
2 large eggs, separated
250ml milk
3 tbsp sunflower oil
125g blueberries

1. Preheat the oven to 180°C (160°C fan) and line a 12-hole muffin tin with paper cases.

2. In a large mixing bowl, combine both flours, rolled oats, baking powder, cinnamon, chia seeds, salt and sugar. Create a well in the centre of the dry ingredients and add the banana, egg yolks, milk and oil. Mix everything gently until a wet batter forms.

3. In a separate bowl, whisk the egg whites until they form soft peaks. Fold the egg whites and blueberries into the muffin batter until everything is mixed evenly.

4. Divide the muffin mix between the paper cases and bake in the oven for 25 minutes, or until golden and firm to the touch.

5. The muffins will keep for 4–5 days in an airtight container. They also freeze well in ziplock freezer bags.

While porridge always steals the show during the winter, summer is all about granola. I love the satisfaction of making up a batch of this, knowing it's ready for breakfast. I eat mine with yoghurt, an extra drizzle of honey and whatever fresh fruit I can get my hands on.

My Favourite Granola

1. Preheat the oven to 160°C (140°C fan).

2. Combine all the dry ingredients in a large mixing bowl, drizzle over the honey and coconut oil and mix until well combined. Tip the contents out onto a large baking tray and spread out evenly.

3. Toast in the oven for approximately 25–30 minutes, but keep an eye on it as ovens vary – you are looking for the oats to just turn a light golden brown. Give the oats a mix halfway through the cooking time to ensure an even colour.

4. Remove from the oven and allow to cool on the tray before transferring to an airtight container. The granola should last up to two weeks (if you don't eat it all before then) and can be served with yoghurt or milk (try soya or almond as an alternative).

Makes enough for 6–8 servings

300g jumbo oats
175g mixed nuts (almonds, pecan or pistachios)
100g pumpkin seeds
50g sunflower seeds
1 tsp ground cinnamon
½ tsp fine sea salt
125g mixed dried fruit (raisins, dried mango, dried apricots)
3 tbsp honey
3 tbsp coconut oil, melted

Breakfast Pep 'n' Power Bars

These breakfast bars are full of goodness and natural sugars – guaranteed to get you off to a good start. The mixture works well cut into bars but can also be rolled into smaller balls.

Makes 8 bars

150g ground almonds
4 tbsp almond butter
2 tbsp 100% cocoa powder
20 medjool dates (approx 525g with stones or 480g without)
150ml espresso, cooled
Pinch of sea salt
2 tbsp chia seeds
150g porridge oats
4 tbsp desiccated coconut

To decorate
Raw cacao nibs
Toasted almonds
Desiccated coconut
Matcha green tea powder

1. Line a 15cm square baking tin with parchment paper.

2. Place the almonds, almond butter, cocoa powder, dates and espresso in a food processor with a pinch of sea salt and blitz until you have a smooth mixture.

3. Using a spatula fold through the chia seeds, oats and desiccated coconut. Tip the mixture into the lined tin and press and flatten it. Stud the top with cacao nibs, almonds, coconut and matcha powder (use some or all of the above as you choose) and then chill in the fridge for 1 hour.

4. Remove from the tin, peel off the parchment paper and slice into bars. Wrap in small sheets of parchment paper and tie with string for a bar on the go!

4 Ways Breakfast Toast Toppers

Sun-dried Tomato Pesto

Serves 4
250g sun-dried tomatoes
75g skinless almonds
1 garlic clove, finely chopped
100ml extra-virgin olive oil
3 tbsp balsamic vinegar
1 tsp cayenne pepper
Sea salt

1. Place all the ingredients in a food processor and blitz until you have a smooth pesto. If the mixture is too thick, loosen with a little more olive oil.

2. Spread on toast or spoon into a serving bowl.

Guacamole

Serves 4–6
2 firm, ripe avocados
1 garlic clove, finely chopped
Juice of ½ lime, plus lime wedges to serve
1–2 dashes of Tabasco sauce
Small handful of fresh coriander, roughly chopped, plus a few leaves to garnish
Sea salt and freshly ground black pepper

1. Slice each avocado in half, remove the stone, then spoon out the flesh into a bowl. Add the garlic, lime juice and Tabasco, then mash with the back of a fork. (You could also do your mashing using a pestle and mortar if you wish.)

2. When you have a rough mash, stir through the chopped coriander. Season well with salt and pepper, then spread on toast or spoon into a serving bowl. Garnish with coriander.

Having something smooth and creamy, yet booming with exciting colour and vibrant flavours, to spread on a piece of sourdough toast or crusty bread can make a great breakfast.

Chickpea Hummus

Serves 6

2 x 400g tins chickpeas, rinsed and drained
1 garlic clove, finely chopped
1 tbsp tahini
1 tsp ground cumin
1 tsp smoked paprika
Pinch of cayenne pepper, plus extra to serve
Juice of ½ lemon
Sea salt
Extra-virgin olive oil, for drizzling

1. Tip the chickpeas into a food processor and add the garlic, tahini, cumin, paprika, cayenne pepper, lemon juice and enough sea salt to taste. Blitz until smooth; if it looks a little too stiff, simply loosen it with a little water.

2. Spread on toast or spoon into a serving bowl and serve with a drizzle of extra-virgin olive oil and a sprinkling of cayenne pepper.

Beetroot Hummus

Serves 6

4 cooked beetroot
1 garlic clove, roughly chopped
2 tsp ground cumin
2 tbsp pomegranate molasses, plus extra to drizzle
1 tbsp tahini
Juice of 1 lemon, plus extra if needed
Sea salt and freshly ground black pepper
2 tbsp toasted sesame seeds, to serve

1. Blitz all the ingredients together, except for the sesame seeds, in a food processor until smooth. Season with salt and pepper and add a little more lemon juice to taste, if required.

2. Spread on toast or spoon into a serving bowl. Drizzle with a little more pomegranate molasses and sprinkle with the toasted sesame seeds.

4 Ways Overnight Oats

Soaking oats overnight changes their consistency and makes them much softer. I've added chia seeds here for their jelly texture, which makes this breakfast more like a fancy dessert!

Raspberry and Almond

Serves 1

25g rolled oats

1 tbsp chia seeds

150ml almond milk

80g raspberries

Coconut or natural yoghurt, to serve

1 tbsp toasted flaked almonds

1. Combine the oats, chia seeds and almond milk in a jar with a tight-fitting lid and place in the fridge overnight.

2. Blitz half the raspberries with a hand-held stick blender until smooth. If you are warming the oats, heat the soaked oats gently in a small pan. Stir through the puréed raspberries and top with a generous dollop of yoghurt, the remaining whole raspberries and the toasted flaked almonds.

Blueberry and Lemon

Serves 1

25g rolled oats

1 tbsp chia seeds

150ml almond milk

40g blueberries

Coconut or natural yoghurt, to serve

Zest of ½ lemon

1. Combine the oats, chia seeds and almond milk in a jar with a tight-fitting lid and place in the fridge overnight.

2. Blitz the blueberries with a hand-held stick blender until smooth. If you are warming the oats, heat the soaked oats gently in a small pan. Swirl the puréed blueberries through the oats and top with a generous dollop of yoghurt and the grated lemon zest.

Strawberry and Chocolate

Serves 1

25g rolled oats

1 tbsp chia seeds

150ml almond milk

1 tbsp honey

1 tsp cocoa powder

80g strawberries, hulled

Coconut or natural yoghurt, to serve

1 tbsp raw cacao nibs

1. Combine the oats, chia seeds and almond milk in a jar with a tight-fitting lid and place in the fridge overnight.

2. Mix together the honey and cocoa powder and set aside. Blitz half the strawberries with a hand-held stick blender until smooth. If you are warming the oats, heat the soaked oats gently in a small pan. Stir through the puréed strawberries and top with a generous dollop of yoghurt, the remaining strawberries, a drizzle of the chocolate sauce and the cacao nibs.

Totally Tropical

Serves 1

25g rolled oats

1 tbsp chia seeds

150ml almond milk

1 ripe mango, peeled and thinly sliced

Coconut or natural yoghurt, to serve

1 tsp desiccated coconut

Honey, for drizzling

1. Combine the oats, chia seeds and almond milk in a jar with a tight-fitting lid and place in the fridge overnight.

2. Blitz half of the mango with a hand-held stick blender until smooth. If you are warming the oats, heat the soaked oats gently in a small pan. Stir the smooth mango through the soaked oats and top with a generous dollop of yoghurt, the rest of the sliced mango, desiccated coconut and a drizzle of honey.

Apple, Cinnamon and Pecan Porridge

I am a creature of comfort and repetition: while there are many regular breakfast dishes that fall in and out of favour, I will always come back to this porridge with shredded apple and cinnamon. A warm hug in a bowl, this is the kind of thing you need to soothe you during the colder months of the year. I use milk in my porridge but you can use water instead.

Serves 1–2

75g porridge oats
350ml milk, or water if you prefer, plus extra to serve (optional)
Pinch of salt
1 eating apple
1 tsp ground cinnamon, plus extra to serve
2 tbsp honey, plus a drizzle to serve
Small handful of toasted pecans, roughly chopped

1. Put the porridge and milk in a pan. Place over a medium–high heat and bring to the boil, then reduce the heat to low. Add a pinch of salt and stir continuously until you have a thick, creamy mixture – this will take roughly 8 minutes.

2. Grate the apple (including the skin) and stir half of it into the cooked porridge, then add the cinnamon and honey and mix well.

3. Pour the porridge into a bowl then top it with the rest of the grated apple, some more cinnamon and honey. Scatter the toasted pecans over the top. It's a nice little addition to add some cold milk over the top if you like.

These semolina pancakes are brilliant for anyone with a dairy intolerance as they don't contain milk – if you skip the yoghurt and honey to serve they can also be vegan- friendly. Inspired by one of my favourite Dublin brunch spots, Brother Hubbard, these pancakes are light and particularly good served with slow-roasted rhubarb, yoghurt and mint.

Semolina Pancakes with Slow-roasted Rhubarb, Yoghurt and Pistachios

1. Put the semolina, yeast, baking powder, caster sugar, flour and salt in a food processor. Add the lukewarm water and whizz to a smooth batter. Pour the batter into a bowl, cover and set aside in a warm place for 45 minutes, or until the batter has doubled in size and become frothy.

2. Place a large frying pan over a medium-high heat. When hot brush with a little oil. Add a scant ladleful of the batter to the pan (you should fit about 3 pancakes in the pan) and cook for 2 minutes, or until little bubbles appear on the surface. Flip and cook on the other side until golden brown. Remove from the pan and repeat the process with the remaining batter.

3. Arrange 2–3 pancakes per person on a plate and top with a dollop of yoghurt and a couple of rhubarb pieces. Drizzle with honey and scatter over a few chopped pistachios and mint leaves.

Serves 4–6

375g fine semolina
7g fast-action dried yeast
2 tsp baking powder
2 tbsp caster sugar
1 tbsp plain flour
1 tsp salt
750ml lukewarm water
Vegetable oil, to brush

To serve
4 tbsp natural yoghurt
Fragrant Roasted Rhubarb (see page 150)
Honey, for drizzling
Handful of chopped pistachios
Few mint leaves, torn

Gluten-free Pancakes with Blueberry, Banana and Honey

I've been making variations of these pancakes for years and the basic batter can be adapted with the addition of all sorts of ingredients such as nuts, seeds, chocolate and berries. Store-bought oat flour can be used here, but I normally blitz up oats in a food processor until they are a fine consistency.

Serves 2

120g oat flour (oats blitzed in food processor)
1 tsp gluten-free baking powder
1 tbsp chia seeds, flax seeds or ground pumpkin seeds
Pinch of fine sea salt
100ml milk
2 large free-range eggs, separated
150g blueberries
1 tbsp coconut oil
1 large ripe banana, peeled and sliced
Honey, coconut yoghurt and bee pollen, to serve

1. Place all the dry ingredients in a large mixing bowl, mix to combine and then make a well in the centre. Pour the milk in a jug and add the egg yolks. Whisk lightly to combine. Add to the dry ingredients and mix until blended.

2. In a clean bowl, whisk the egg whites until they hold soft peaks. Fold gently into the batter until combined. Add a handful of the blueberries to the batter if you want and fold in.

3. To cook the pancakes, melt the coconut oil in a large frying pan over a medium heat and add a small ladleful of the mixture to the hot pan. Cook for about 2–3 minutes on each side, or until the pancakes are golden brown. Serve the pancakes on warm plates with banana slices, blueberries, a drizzle of honey, yoghurt and bee pollen.

One of my favourite breakfasts in the whole world is Eggs Benedict – I find it pretty hard to resist if I spot it on a breakfast menu. Traditionally it's a ridiculously rich dish with a butter-laden sauce (no wonder it tastes good!), but I have been making a great alternative which swaps the stodgy English muffin with a crispy sweet potato rösti, bumps up the nutrition with some pan-fried spinach and cuts out the butter by making a healthier hollandaise. The inspiration for the ludicrously delicious hollandaise comes from Indy Power who writes The Little Green Spoon, a fantastic healthy-eating Irish food blog.

Poached Egg, Sweet Potato Rösti and Healthy Hollandaise

1. Preheat the oven to 200°C (180°C fan).

2. Start with the sweet potato rösti. Place the grated sweet potato in a large bowl and crack in the egg. Season with salt and black pepper and stir well to combine. Place a large, ovenproof frying pan over a medium-high heat and add the coconut oil. Place 4 heaped tablespoons of the mixture into the hot oil and press down to create little flat cakes. Fry until golden and then flip to the other side. Place the whole pan in the oven for 15–20 minutes, until cooked all the way through.

3. For the healthy hollandaise, fill a blender with boiling water while you prepare the rest of the sauce ingredients. Pour out the water when you are ready to start. The heat of the blender will help the sauce emulsify and thicken. Add the egg yolks and lemon juice, then blitz until smooth. While the mixer is still on slowly add in the melted coconut oil until the sauce is smooth and slightly thickened, then season.

4. To poach the eggs, fill a pan with about 5cm of water, then bring to the boil. Add a pinch of sea salt and the vinegar. Lower the heat to a very gentle simmer and drop the eggs into the water right at the surface (you may find it easier to break each egg into a cup and slide it gently into the water). Cook for 3–4 minutes before removing with a slotted spoon and draining on kitchen paper.

5. Meanwhile, cook the spinach. Melt the coconut oil in a large frying pan over a medium-high heat and wilt the spinach. Season with salt and pepper. Drain off any excess water and keep warm. To serve, place the sweet potato rösti on four plates, divide the spinach between them and top each with a poached egg. Pour over a generous amount of the hollandaise sauce, scatter with the chopped chives and a grinding of black pepper.

Serves 4

4 large free-range eggs
1 tbsp white wine vinegar
2 tsp coconut oil
150g spinach, tough stalks removed
Small handful of fresh chives, finely chopped
Sea salt and freshly ground black pepper

For the sweet potato rösti
1 large sweet potato (or 2 smaller ones), coarsely grated
1 large free-range egg
3 tbsp coconut oil
Sea salt and freshly ground black pepper

For the healthy hollandaise
2 egg yolks
Juice of ½ lemon
3 tbsp melted coconut oil
Sea salt and freshly ground black pepper

Huevos Rancheros Scrambled Eggs

This sort of breakfast, even though Mexican-inspired, always reminds me of Los Angeles, where they do really good Huevos Rancheros. The dish is normally comprised of fried eggs with crispy corn tortillas, refried beans, guacamole, and a tomato salsa. This a quick and easy way of taking those fantastic Mexican flavours and transforming them into a fast and fresh breakfast.

Serves 2

4 large free-range eggs, lightly beaten
6 small corn tortillas, warmed in the oven
½ quantity of Guacamole (see page 26)
Sea salt and freshly ground black pepper

For the tomato salsa
200g cherry tomatoes, diced
½ red onion, finely chopped
Small handful of fresh coriander, roughly chopped, plus a few sprigs to garnish
Juice of ½ lime, plus wedges to garnish
Sea salt, to taste

1. Prepare the tomato salsa by combining all the ingredients together in a bowl. Season with sea salt to taste. Set aside at room temperature until needed.

2. Heat a small non-stick pan over a medium-high heat and add the eggs. Lower the heat and scramble the eggs slowly until you have a thick but loose scrambled egg mixture. Remove from the heat immediately and season with sea salt and ground black pepper.

3. To serve, smear each corn tortilla with a heaped tablespoon of the Guacamole. Spoon the scrambled eggs on top, then scatter over the tomato salsa. Garnish with coriander sprigs and lime wedges.

Za'atar Quinoa Poached Eggs

On a cold New York morning a few years ago while searching for food inspiration, I got to visit a great little café called Buvette on the trendy East Side. Sitting at the marble bar listening to the hustle and bustle of busy New Yorkers, I had this unusual breakfast dish. Although it doesn't instantly feel like a meal for the start of the day, it makes for a dish that is as comforting as it is nutritious. The sprinkle of za'atar instantly transports the taste buds to the Middle East, while the runny poached egg, mineral-rich greens and quinoa provide long-lasting nourishment.

Serves 2

150g quinoa
350ml vegetable stock
1 tbsp extra-virgin olive oil
110g kale, leaves torn from stem
80g spinach
1 garlic clove, finely sliced
8 cherry tomatoes, halved
3 spring onions, finely sliced
½ tsp cayenne pepper
1 tsp smoked paprika
2 large free-range eggs
Sea salt
1 tbsp white wine vinegar
Za'atar, for sprinkling

1. Place the quinoa and vegetable stock in a pan and place over a medium heat. Bring to the boil, then reduce the heat and simmer for about 15 minutes, or until the quinoa is cooked. Drain and set aside.

2. Heat the olive oil in a large frying pan over a medium–high heat. Add the kale and fry until just softened. Add in the spinach and garlic and fry until the kale and spinach have wilted. Stir through the quinoa, tomatoes, spring onions, cayenne pepper and paprika and season with sea salt. Continue to cook just until the tomatoes have softened slightly.

3. To poach the eggs, fill a pan with about 5cm of water, then bring to the boil. Add a pinch of sea salt and the vinegar. Lower the heat to a very gentle simmer and drop the eggs into the water right at the surface (you may find it easier to break each egg into a cup and slide it gently into the water). Cook for 3–4 minutes before removing with a slotted spoon and draining on kitchen paper.

4. Serve the quinoa topped with the poached eggs and a sprinkle of za'atar.

When I was younger, most Sundays would start with the smell of my dad grilling bacon and sausages. By the time we made it down the stairs, he would be asking how we wanted our eggs – pretty good service now that I think back! As much as the fairly irresistible smell of a traditional Irish fry can be hard to beat, even my dad has cut back on this weekly treat – more often than not the offer is now a green smoothie! But my dad isn't the only one looking for healthy breakfast options, as proved by one of my favourite local restaurants, The House, in my hometown of Howth, which serves up this popular healthy take on the classic fry.

The House Vegetarian Fry

1. Heat about 1 teaspoon of olive oil in a frying pan over a medium-high heat and fry the spinach for about 3–4 minutes, or until it has wilted down. Squeeze out any excess water and keep warm.

2. Place the frying pan back over a medium-high heat with a little more olive oil. Add in the onion and garlic and fry for 5–6 minutes, or until softened. Add the tinned tomatoes and oregano and season with salt and pepper. Bring to the boil, then lower the heat and simmer for 6–8 minutes. Stir through the beans and continue to cook for a further 2 minutes. Transfer to a bowl and keep warm.

3. To 'steam-fry' the eggs, heat about 1 teaspoon of olive oil in a large, non-stick frying pan over a medium-high heat. Crack the eggs into the pan and pour in 3 tablespoons of water. Cover and cook slowly until the white is set and the yolk remains runny.

4. Place a griddle pan over a medium-high heat and brush with a little oil. When hot, add the tomato halves and mushrooms and cook for 3–4 minutes on each side, or until they are tender and have defined griddle marks.

5. Serve the griddled tomatoes and mushrooms with the soda bread toast, quick baked beans, spinach and eggs. Tuck in!

Serves 2

Olive oil
250g spinach
½ red onion, finely chopped
1 garlic clove, chopped
1 x 400g tin plum tomatoes
1 tsp dried oregano
1 x 400g tin cannellini beans, rinsed and drained
2 large free-range eggs
2 fresh plum tomatoes, halved
4 Portobello mushrooms
Sea salt and freshly ground black pepper
2 slices of wholemeal soda bread toast, to serve

Post Workout Omelette

I like the sound of this recipe title, it makes me feel like I'm in the gym more than I possibly am! Workout or no workout, this is a seriously good omelette and one I dig into as often as I can. Mix up the filling as you wish but I love the combination of sweet cherry tomatoes, slightly bitter colourful greens and salty feta cheese.

Serves 1

2 tsp rapeseed oil
2–3 small stalks rainbow chard with leaves, roughly chopped
1 garlic clove, finely minced
3 large free-range eggs
50g feta cheese
100g cherry tomatoes, halved
2 tbsp toasted sesame seeds
Sea salt and freshly ground black pepper

1. Heat 1 teaspoon of the oil in a large, non-stick frying pan over a medium-high heat and fry the chard until it is tender. When the chard is ready, stir through the garlic and continue to fry for another minute. Season to taste and transfer to a plate.

2. Whisk the eggs in a bowl until combined and season with salt and pepper.

3. Place the pan back on the heat with the remaining teaspoon of oil. Pour in the eggs and allow to set briefly before swirling with a spatula. Scatter with the feta cheese, rainbow chard, cherry tomatoes and seeds before folding one half of the omelette over.

4. Slide on to a plate and serve immediately.

4 Ways Super Smoothies

Kick Ass Kale Kleaner

Serves 2
2 large handfuls of kale
480ml freshly pressed apple juice, plus extra if needed
Juice of ½ lime
1 banana, peeled and roughly chopped
Ice cubes, to serve

1. Place all of the ingredients, except the ice, into a smoothie maker and blend until smooth (or use a jug and hand-held stick blender).

2. If it is a little thick, add in a little extra apple juice. Pour into glasses half-filled with ice and serve.

Nutty Mango and Banana Smoothie

Serves 2
225ml freshly squeezed orange juice, plus extra if needed
100ml natural probiotic yoghurt
1 ripe mango, peeled and flesh roughly chopped
1 banana, peeled and roughly chopped
Small handful of oats
1 tbsp almond butter
Ice cubes, to serve

1. Place all of the ingredients, except the ice, into a smoothie maker and blend until smooth (or use a jug and hand-held stick blender).

2. Pour into glasses half-filled with ice to serve.

Smoothies are a great way to get that burst of vitamins you need in the morning, especially when using superfoods like kale (balanced here with zingy lime juice). Frozen fruit smoothies are great for kids, as the vibrant colours look super-appealing. Other fantastic smoothie ingredients include almond butter for added richness and oats to help fill you up for the day.

Frozen Red Velvet

Serves 2

250ml freshly squeezed orange juice, plus extra if needed

225g frozen raspberries

1 banana, peeled and roughly chopped

1 tbsp chia seeds

3 tbsp rolled oats

1. Place all of the ingredients into a smoothie maker and blend until smooth (or use a jug and hand-held stick blender).

2. Add a little extra orange juice if you think it's a bit thick. Pour into glasses to serve.

Totally Tropical Taste Tickler

Serves 2

1 ripe mango, peeled and flesh roughly chopped

175g fresh pineapple chunks

2 tsp freshly grated ginger

500ml coconut water

Juice of 1 lime

Ice cubes, to serve

1. Place all of the ingredients, except the ice, into a smoothie maker and blend until smooth (or use a jug and hand-held stick blender).

2. Pour into glasses half-filled with ice to serve.

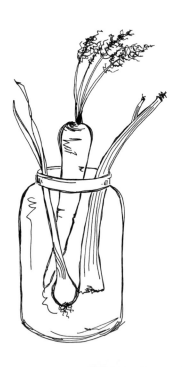

food on the run

I guess you could call this the SOS chapter. It's the one I rely on most heavily when it comes to eating well throughout the day when I'm on the move and it's one that relies most heavily on preparation. One of the things that gets to me most when I'm travelling is not having good food choices on offer. You end up being at the mercy of whatever shop, deli, or (gasp!) petrol station you rock up to. Which is why it's essential to take back control. The majority of the recipes in this chapter fit quite happily into a lunchbox or flask and can be eaten hot or cold, giving you lots of great options for food on the go.

All the salads are crunchy and crisp, ensuring no disappointing sogginess; on the contrary, the salads in this book are more than a little exciting, with recipes like Cucumber Tahini Crunch Noodle Salad, with zingy dressing, toasted sesame seeds and slippery rice noodles, or the Mini Falafel Box with Shredded Salad and Spiced Yoghurt to tickle your taste buds. Recipes like smoky Piri Piri Chicken with Chopped Green Veg Salad Box and crunchy Veggie Summer Rolls with Vietnamese Dipping Sauce can all be made in advance and enjoyed for lunch on the move.

Many of the recipes in this chapter can be made the night before, ensuring you leave the house with every opportunity to eat well throughout the day. Take your time enjoying the preparation and choosing what you want to eat and those better food choices will make themselves. Most importantly, make time to sit down and savour the food while you eat: one of the most important lessons for anyone rushing through a stressful day.

4 Ways Chunky Soups

Carrot and Coriander Noodle Soup

Serves 4–6
900ml chicken stock
2 garlic cloves, thinly sliced
Thumb-sized piece of fresh ginger, peeled and cut into matchsticks
1 mild red chilli, thinly sliced into rings
1 x 400ml tin light coconut milk
225g Thai flat rice noodles
2 large carrots, cut into julienne strips
4 tbsp chopped fresh coriander
1 tbsp light soy sauce
Juice of 1 lime
1 tsp toasted sesame oil

1. Pour the stock into a large pan and add the garlic, ginger and chilli. Bring to the boil, stirring, and then reduce the heat and simmer for 5 minutes until the ginger is nice and tender.

2. Add the coconut milk and rice noodles and cook until the noodles are soft, about 3 minutes.

3. Increase the heat back up to high, stir in the carrots and cook for 2 minutes until the carrots are tender but still have a little bite. Add the coriander (reserving a few leaves to garnish), soy sauce, lime juice and sesame oil and cook for another 20 seconds, then ladle into bowls. Scatter with the remaining coriander and serve.

Winter Root Vegetable Soup

Serves 6–8
1 tbsp butter
1 onion, chopped
1 leek, sliced
2 potatoes, peeled and chopped
2 litres vegetable stock
2 carrots, chopped
1 parsnip, chopped
1 small celeriac, peeled and chopped
Sea salt and freshly ground black pepper
Sliced brown soda bread, to serve (optional)

1. Put the butter in a large pan and place over a medium-high heat. As soon as the butter has melted and is foaming, add the onion, leek and potatoes. Sauté for 2 minutes, then cover the pan, reduce the heat and sweat for 8 minutes.

2. Add the stock to the pan along with the carrots, parsnip and celeriac, then lower the heat and simmer for about 20 minutes, or until the vegetables are completely tender. Season to taste and then ladle into bowls. Serve with slices of brown soda bread, if liked.

I love soup's endless possibilities and these four are a perfect testament to just that. These are a really great way to get fresh vegetables into your diet.

Spring Vegetable Minestrone

Serves 4

2 tbsp extra-virgin olive oil, plus extra to drizzle
1 bunch of spring onions, trimmed and finely chopped
2 garlic cloves, thinly sliced
1 fennel bulb, trimmed, halved and finely chopped
200g mixed green vegetables (such as asparagus, courgettes, green beans, peas, and broad beans)
100g spaghetti, broken up into small pieces
700ml vegetable stock (from a cube is ok)
2 tbsp basil pesto
Sea salt and freshly ground black pepper
Chopped fresh basil and flat-leaf parsley, to garnish

1. Heat the olive oil in a large pan over a medium heat. Add the spring onions, garlic and fennel and gently sauté for about 10 minutes without allowing them to colour.

2. Meanwhile, prepare the green vegetables, depending on what you have – remove the woody ends from asparagus and finely slice the stalks (leave the tips whole) and trim and finely chop courgettes and green beans.

3. Tip all the prepared green vegetables into the pan, then add the broken spaghetti and stock. Bring to the boil, then simmer for about 10 minutes, or until the spaghetti is just tender. Season with a little salt and pepper.

4. Ladle into big bowls and add a heaped teaspoonful of pesto. Scatter with chopped basil and parsley and drizzle with a little extra-virgin olive oil to serve.

Poached Chicken Noodle Soup

Serves 6–8

1.2kg whole organic chicken
2 onions, chopped
2 carrots, chopped
2 celery sticks, chopped
2 large garlic cloves, thinly sliced
Few thyme sprigs
2 fresh bay leaves
225g rice vermicelli noodles, broken into small pieces
Small handful each of fresh flat-leaf parsley and dill, finely chopped
Sea salt and freshly ground black pepper

1. Put the chicken into a large stockpot. Cover with cold water and place over a medium-high heat. Once the water comes to the boil, reduce the heat and simmer for 30 minutes, skimming off any froth that rises to the surface.

2. Add all the vegetables to the chicken with the garlic and herbs, then season generously with salt. Bring back to the boil, then reduce the heat and simmer for 1 hour, adding the noodles for the last 10 minutes. Continue to skim the broth as necessary. Carefully remove the chicken from the pot, using tongs. Transfer to a roasting tin and leave until cool enough to handle.

3. Shred the meat off the carcass, discarding the skin and bones. Add the shredded chicken back into the soup with the parsley and dill, then allow to warm through. Season to taste with salt and pepper and ladle into bowls to serve.

Rainbow Beetroot Salad

You can get great beetroot these days – in fantastic colours. It is in season from June until the end of February so keep an eye out for it at your local farmers' market. All it needs is a light wash or peel depending on its size. Use a swivel vegetable peeler to pare it into wafer-thin slices. The horseradish will help soften it and helps to give the salad a nice kick.

Serves 4

2 oranges
200g cooked red quinoa (see page 214)
½ head Savoy cabbage, tough stalks removed and leaves roughly shredded
4 raw beetroot (in various colours), peeled and pared into wafer-thin slices
1 large ripe avocado, peeled, stoned and cut into bite-sized pieces
2 roasted red peppers in oil (from a jar), drained and cut into bite-sized pieces

For the turmeric dressing
½ tsp ground turmeric
1 tsp freshly grated horseradish (or from a jar is fine)
2 tsp honey
Juice of ½ lemon
2 tbsp extra-virgin olive oil
Sea salt and freshly ground black pepper

1. Use a sharp knife to cut away the peel and white pith from the oranges. Cut the oranges into segments, holding them over a bowl to catch the juices, which you will use for the dressing.

2. Put the red quinoa into a large bowl and fold in the orange segments with the Savoy cabbage, shaved beetroots, avocado and roasted red peppers.

3. To make the dressing, add the turmeric, horseradish, honey, and lemon juice to the leftover orange juice (you should have about 1–2 tablespoons) and then whisk in the olive oil. Season with salt and pepper. Fold into the salad and arrange on plates to serve.

Tahini Crunch Noodle Salad

This fresh crunchy noodle salad relies on the creamy richness from a simple satay dressing to bring it to life. I often make double this recipe for a quick and light supper; the rest makes a great lunchbox filler the following day.

Serves 4

2 carrots
2 large cucumbers
2 large handfuls of kale (about 100g), leaves torn from stem and roughly chopped
5 spring onions, finely sliced
200g cooked flat rice noodles
4 tbsp sesame seeds, toasted
Small handful of fresh coriander, roughly chopped
Small handful of fresh mint, roughly chopped

For the tahini dressing
1 chilli, finely chopped
1 garlic clove, finely chopped
Thumb-sized piece of fresh ginger, peeled and finely chopped
3 tbsp tahini
1 tbsp soy sauce
1 tsp sesame oil, plus extra for massaging the kale

1. Peel the carrots into long ribbons using a vegetable peeler. Do the same with the cucumbers, but turn the cucumbers and peel from the other side when you reach the seeds in the middle (discard the seeds).

2. Whisk together the ingredients for the dressing and loosen with a few tablespoons of water until it reaches the consistency of single cream. The dressing keeps well in the fridge for up to 5 days.

3. In a large mixing bowl, massage the kale (see page 54) with a small drizzle of sesame oil until it is tender. Add the carrots, cucumber, half the spring onions, noodles, half the sesame seeds, coriander and mint.

4. Pour over the dressing and toss until all the ingredients are evenly coated. Scatter over the remaining sesame seeds and spring onions to serve. This salad is great enjoyed straight away but will also keep well if made in advance.

Nutty Kale Salad with Red Cabbage, Mango and Sesame Dressing

You may have heard of 'massaging' kale and wondered what all the fuss was about. Massaging raw kale transforms it from a tough, somewhat bitter leaf into a sweet delicate salad and it only takes a few minutes! The combination of lime juice and salt helps to break down the cell walls in the kale, softening it and making it sweeter. So show your kale a bit of love…

Serves 4

400g curly kale, tough stems removed and torn into bite-sized pieces
1 tbsp lime juice
½ red cabbage, tough stalk removed, finely shredded
1 firm ripe mango, peeled, stoned and cut into thin strips
1 mild red chilli, deseeded and thinly sliced
15g fresh mint, leaves picked and roughly chopped
20g fresh coriander, leaves picked and roughly chopped
25g toasted flaked almonds
2 tbsp toasted sesame seeds
Sea salt

For the dressing

2 tbsp light olive oil
1 tbsp toasted sesame oil
2 tbsp lime juice
1 tbsp maple syrup
1 tsp soy sauce
Sea salt and freshly ground black pepper

1. Place the kale in a large bowl with the lime juice and a good pinch of salt and massage for 5 minutes. Add the red cabbage, mango, chilli, mint and coriander, stirring gently to combine.

2. To make the dressing, put the olive oil, sesame oil, lime juice, maple syrup and soy sauce in a small bowl and whisk until thickened, then season with salt and pepper. Fold the dressing into the kale salad and scatter over the almonds and sesame seeds to serve.

4 Ways Blitzed Soups

Red Lentil and Sweet Potato Soup

Serves 4–6

1 tbsp olive oil
1 small onion, finely chopped
1 carrot, finely chopped
1 celery stick, finely chopped
Good pinch of ground allspice
1 tsp fresh thyme leaves, plus extra to garnish
1–2 red birds' eye chillies, deseeded and finely chopped
1 large sweet potato, peeled and diced
75g split red lentils
900ml chicken or vegetable stock (from a cube is ok)
4–6 tbsp crème fraîche
Sea salt and freshly ground black pepper

1. Heat the olive oil in a large pan over a medium heat and sauté the onion, carrot and celery for 5 minutes, until softened but not coloured.

2. Add the allspice, thyme and enough chilli to your liking and stir for 1 minute. Add the sweet potato, lentils and stock. Bring to the boil, then season with salt and pepper. Reduce the heat back to medium, cover and simmer for 20 minutes, until the sweet potato and lentils are completely tender.

3. Purée the soup with a hand-held stick blender, then ladle into bowls and add a dollop of crème fraîche to each one. Garnish with a little sprinkling of thyme leaves and a good grinding of pepper to serve.

Carrot and Cardamom Soup with Nuts and Seeds

Serves 4–6

2 tbsp olive oil
1 large onion, thinly sliced
5 cardamom pods
Thumb-sized piece of fresh ginger, peeled
675g carrots, grated
1 tbsp clear honey
1 tsp lemon juice
900ml boiling water
Sea salt and freshly ground black pepper
Handful of mixed nuts and seeds, to serve

1. Heat the oil in a large pan over a medium heat and add the onion, stirring to coat in the oil – don't let the onions take any colour.

2. Using the flat blade of a heavy knife, lightly crush the cardamom pods and remove the seeds (discard the pods). Crush the ginger in the same way, which helps to release the juice. Add the ginger and cardamom seeds to the onion and leave to sweat for 10 minutes, stirring occasionally.

3. Add the carrots, honey and lemon juice and season generously with salt and pepper. Pour in the boiling water, bring it back to the boil, then reduce the heat and simmer for 45 minutes, until the carrots are tender.

4. Blitz with a hand-held stick blender until smooth and creamy. Ladle into bowls and scatter each one with a sprinkling of the mixed nuts and seeds.

Blitzed soups like these are perfect for a lunch on the move, all of them can easily be transferred to a flask and kept warm until you're ready for them. Even though they are blitzed until silky smooth, they are all full of vibrant flavours and nutrient-packed vegetables to keep you going.

Super Green Pea Soup

Serves 6

1 small ham hock
2 tbsp olive oil
1 bunch spring onions, trimmed and finely chopped
450g frozen peas
450g frozen spinach
600ml vegetable stock
Few mint sprigs, leaves picked and roughly chopped
Sea salt and freshly ground black pepper

1. Place the ham hock in a large pan, then cover with cold water and bring to the boil. Skim off any froth that rises to the surface. Reduce the heat and simmer for about 45 minutes, or until the meat starts to pull away from the bone. Remove from the heat and leave the hock to cool in the liquid.

2. Once the ham hock has cooled down, remove it from the pan and set aside. Reserve 600ml of the cooking liquid and discard the rest.

3. Clean the pan, add the olive oil and place over a medium heat. Add the spring onions and sauté for 2–3 minutes until softened but not coloured. Add the peas, spinach, stock and reserved ham liquid and stir well to combine. Bring to the boil and then reduce the heat and simmer for 5 minutes.

4. Using a hand-held stick blender, blitz the peas in the pan. When the soup is almost smooth, add the mint and continue to blitz until smooth. Add a little more stock if the soup is too thick. Season to taste with salt and pepper (you won't need to add much salt as the ham hock liquid will be quite salty).

5. Remove the skin from the ham hock, cut up the meat and add this to the soup, then allow to warm through. Ladle into bowls to serve.

Tomato and Chickpea Soup

Serves 4–6

200g raw chorizo sausage, halved lengthways and sliced
1 large onion, chopped
225g celery, chopped
300g carrots, chopped
2 garlic cloves, finely chopped
1 tsp smoked paprika
1 tsp mild chilli powder
½ tsp ground cumin
1 x 400g tin chopped tomatoes
750ml vegetable stock (from a cube is OK)
1 x 400g tin chickpeas, drained and rinsed
Sea salt and freshly ground black pepper
Extra-virgin olive oil and chopped fresh flat-leaf parsley, to garnish

1. Fry the chorizo in a large pan over a medium heat until it is golden and has released its lovely spicy oil. Remove with a slotted spoon and set aside.

2. Add the onion, celery and carrots to the chorizo oil in the pan, reduce the heat and gently fry for another 3–4 minutes. Add the garlic, paprika, chilli powder and cumin and fry for a further minute. Add the tomatoes and stock, stir well and season with a little salt and pepper.

3. Add the chorizo and chickpeas to the pan, holding back a handful for a garnish, and bring to the boil. Reduce the heat and simmer for 10–15 minutes, then blitz with a hand-held stick blender until smooth. Ladle into bowls and add a drizzle of extra-virgin olive oil, the reserved chorizo and chickpeas, a good grinding of black pepper, and a little chopped fresh flat-leaf parsley to serve.

This has to be the perfect transportable feast. If you're making this the night before there is no need to refrigerate the falafels – just leave them covered at room temperature. The spiced yoghurt is great to have with almost anything.

1. To make the falafel, place the red onion, mint, coriander, tahini, lemon zest and juice, cumin, cayenne and paprika in a food processor with a good pinch of salt. Pulse until finely chopped. Add the chickpeas and pulse again briefly until the chickpeas are chopped fine – you are not looking for a smooth paste but something with a bit more texture.

2. With dampened hands, shape into 20 small balls and chill in the fridge for up to an hour (if time allows). Heat a thin film of olive oil in a large non-stick frying pan over a medium heat and fry the falafel balls for 4–6 minutes, until golden brown all over, turning occasionally with tongs. Drain on kitchen paper.

3. To prepare the shredded salad, place all the vegetables in a bowl. Make a quick dressing by whisking together the olive oil, lemon juice, honey and a little salt and pepper (or shake in a jar with a tight-fitting lid) and then use to dress the salad, tossing until evenly coated.

4. To make the spiced yoghurt, mix all the ingredients together in a bowl. Arrange the falafel on the bulgur wheat with a small bowl of the spiced yoghurt. Serve the shredded salad alongside.

Mini Falafel Box

Serves 4

For the falafels
½ small red onion, chopped
Small handful each of fresh mint and coriander leaves
1 tbsp tahini
Zest and juice of ½ lemon
1 tsp ground cumin
1 tsp cayenne pepper
1 tsp smoked paprika
1 x 400g tin chickpeas, drained and rinsed
Olive oil, for frying
Cooked bulgur wheat (see page 214), to serve

For the shredded salad
½ small head of red cabbage, shredded
2 carrots, thinly sliced
½ small red onion, very thinly sliced
3 tbsp extra-virgin olive oil
Juice of ½ lemon
1 tsp honey
Sea salt and freshly ground black pepper

For the spiced yoghurt
1 tsp each of ground coriander and cumin
½ tsp each of ground turmeric and mustard seeds
½ tsp chilli powder
250g natural yoghurt
1 mild red chilli, thinly sliced
3 spring onions, thinly sliced
Sea salt and freshly ground black pepper

Grilled Halloumi Wraps

These wraps are absolutely delicious and perfect for vegetarians. The halloumi can also be cooked on a barbecue. Feel free to experiment with other crunchy salad ingredients, depending on what you have to hand.

Serves 2

2 wholewheat flatbreads (see page 205 or use shop-bought)
2 heaped tbsp Sriracha Yoghurt (see page 107)
100g cooked quinoa (see page 214)
1 Little Gem lettuce, trimmed and shredded
1 ripe avocado, peeled, stoned and chopped
Handful of fresh basil leaves

For the grilled halloumi
250g halloumi, thickly sliced
Olive oil, for brushing
Pinch of dried chilli flakes

For the cherry tomatoes
100g cherry tomatoes, halved
1 tbsp extra-virgin olive oil
1 tsp balsamic vinegar
Sea salt and freshly ground black pepper

1. Start by preparing the cherry tomatoes. Preheat the oven to 190°C (170°C fan) and put the cherry tomatoes into a small roasting tin, cut side up. Drizzle over the olive oil and balsamic vinegar and then season with salt and pepper. Roast for about 45 minutes, until the tomatoes have reduced in size and are slightly charred. Leave to cool at room temperature.

2. When you are almost ready to serve, place a large, non-stick frying pan over a medium-high heat. Brush the slices of halloumi with the olive oil and then sprinkle with the dried chilli flakes. Cook for 2 minutes on each side, or until golden. Transfer to a plate.

3. Wipe out the frying pan and quickly sear each wholewheat wrap for about 10 seconds on each side. Remove from the pan and then smear a tablespoon of Sriracha Yoghurt down the middle of each one. Spoon over the cooked quinoa, then scatter with the shredded lettuce, followed by the avocado and cooled cherry tomatoes. Tear over the basil and finally add the grilled halloumi. Wrap up tightly and then cut each wrap in half and serve immediately.

This is one of my favourite lunchboxes, a really tasty substantial dish that makes the most of leftover chicken. Of course, if you are looking for the ultimate quick fix use vac-packed cooked beetroots and a tin of Puy lentils.

Roasted Beetroot, Lentil and Chicken Lunchbox

1. Preheat the oven to 200°C (180°C fan).

2. Trim any leaves and stalks from the beetroot and place in a roasting tin. Drizzle over the rapeseed oil and scatter with the lemon zest and thyme sprigs; toss to coat. Cover the whole tin with foil and roast in the oven for about 45 minutes or so, depending on the size of the beetroot. When ready, the beetroot should be tender when pierced with a fork. Leave to cool completely, then remove the skin with your fingers or a paring knife. Slice the flesh into bite-sized pieces.

3. In a large bowl, whisk together the ingredients for the dressing and season with salt and pepper. Stir in the red onion and sun-dried tomatoes.

4. Place the lentils in a pan and fill up with water, then place over a high heat and bring to the boil. Reduce the heat and simmer for 20 minutes, until tender. Drain and rinse under cold water, then add the lentils to the bowl with the dressing.

5. Add the roasted beetroot and herbs and toss to combine. Divide among shallow bowls or transportable containers and scatter the roast chicken on top. Stir the lemon juice into the Sriracha Yoghurt and drizzle over to serve.

Serves 4

450g raw whole beetroots
1 tbsp rapeseed oil
Zest and juice of 1 lemon
6 fresh thyme sprigs
1 small red onion, finely diced
100g sun-dried tomatoes, drained and finely chopped
250g Puy lentils
Large handful each of coriander, mint and flat-leaf parsley
Shredded, cooked meat from ½ medium chicken (about 500g)
4 tbsp Sriracha Yoghurt (see page 107)

For the dressing
2 tbsp extra-virgin olive oil
1 tbsp balsamic vinegar
1 garlic clove, very finely chopped
1 tsp Dijon mustard
Sea salt and freshly ground black pepper

Curry Chicken Salad Jar

As kitsch as they may be, these curry chicken salad jars are great to have on the go. Your lunch partner may mock but you can eat away, safe in the knowledge that deep down they're completely jealous. Mix and match the vegetables as you like and make sure you don't overfill the jars to allow for shaking. You'll need a couple of large jars with tight-fitting lids (Kilner jars or recycled pickle jars are ideal).

Serves 2

1 tsp olive oil
2 skinless chicken breast fillets (about 150g each)
3 fresh thyme sprigs, leaves picked
1 large carrot, cut into julienne strips
2 celery sticks, finely diced
4 spring onions, finely sliced
2 large handfuls of salad leaves (rocket, baby spinach, baby kale, Little Gem)
Large handful of toasted almonds, roughly chopped
Sea salt and freshly ground black pepper

For the dressing
4 tbsp natural yoghurt
1 tsp white wine vinegar
Juice of ½ lemon
2 tsp honey
1 tbsp curry powder
1 garlic clove, very finely chopped

1. Heat the oil in a large frying pan over a medium-high heat. Season the chicken with salt and pepper and sprinkle with the thyme leaves. Fry for 4–6 minutes on each side, or until cooked all the way through. Remove from the pan, slice into bite-sized chunks and set aside to cool.

2. Whisk together all the ingredients for the dressing in a bowl and then add the chicken pieces, tossing to coat in the dressing.

3. Place a layer of chicken, carrot, celery, spring onions, salad leaves and toasted almonds in each jar, making sure not to pack everything too tightly. When you are ready to eat, shake the jar to coat the contents. If you find eating straight from the jar a step too far, just tumble the contents out onto a plate when it's time to serve.

Piri Piri Chicken with Chopped Green Veg Salad Box

If you plan on transporting this meal or want to make it in advance, leave the avocado intact until you are ready to eat; otherwise it may discolour.

Serves 4–6

2 tbsp extra-virgin olive oil
1 tsp smoked paprika
½ tsp chopped fresh thyme
1 large garlic clove, crushed
8 boneless chicken thighs (skin on), well trimmed
Sea salt and freshly ground black pepper

For the piri piri sauce
1 large red onion, peeled and sliced in half
2 vine-ripened tomatoes, halved
3 garlic cloves
4 long fresh chillies
1 tbsp red wine vinegar
3 tbsp extra-virgin olive oil, plus extra for griddling
2 thyme sprigs
1 tsp smoked paprika

For the chopped salad
4 spring onions, finely chopped
½ cucumber, chopped
2 small ripe avocados, stoned and chopped
2 Little Gem lettuces, chopped
Large handful of sprouts, cress etc.
1 tsp balsamic vinegar
2 tbsp extra-virgin olive oil

1. Mix 1 tablespoon of the olive oil with the paprika, thyme and garlic and salt and pepper, then rub all over the flesh side of the chicken thighs.

2. Place a large heavy-based frying pan over a medium heat. Add the remaining oil to the pan, then add the chicken thighs, skin side down. Reduce the heat to very low and cook for 20–30 minutes until the skin is nice and crispy. Don't touch them while they are cooking or shake the pan, just leave them alone and you will produce the most fantastic crisp skin and succulent flesh. Turn the chicken thighs and leave to rest in the pan with the heat off for 10 minutes before carving into slices.

3. Meanwhile, make the piri piri sauce. Place a griddle pan over a high heat while you toss the onion, tomatoes, garlic and chillies in a little oil. When the pan is smoking hot, add the vegetables and char on all sides until softened and caramelised. Transfer to a food processor along with the vinegar, olive oil, thyme and paprika and process until smooth. Season to taste with salt and pepper.

4. To make the chopped green salad, place the spring onions, cucumber, avocados, cress and lettuce in a bowl and drizzle over the balsamic and olive oil, then season with salt and pepper. Toss to coat and then divide between your plates or lunchboxes. Top with the sliced chicken thighs and serve with a bowl of the piri piri sauce.

Most large supermarkets now stock Asian foods, such as rice paper wrappers. Keep them as a store cupboard ingredient as they are great for a last minute starter or snack – all you do is soak them in hot water and fill with your favourite ingredients. This recipe is a traditional one, but you can treat rice paper wrappers as the vehicle for a whole host of healthy ingredients. Fill with a selection of finely sliced greens, avocado, red cabbage, nuts and seeds, hot smoked salmon or beans. The dipping sauce is an essential part of enjoying Vietnamese summer rolls, relying on that subtle combination of salty, sweet and spicy. I've added extra herbs, which isn't necessarily traditional but adds an extra layer to this wonderful sauce.

Veggie Summer Rolls with Vietnamese Dipping Sauce

1. First make the dipping sauce. Mix the lime juice, sugar and 100ml water in a small bowl, stirring to dissolve the sugar. Add the fish sauce, garlic and chillies. Taste and adjust the flavours if necessary to balance out the sweet and sour. Cover with cling film and set aside at room temperature until needed.

2. Devein the prawns if necessary: if there is a black line down the back of the prawn use a small, sharp knife to make a shallow cut along the length of the line and carefully lift it out using the tip of the knife.

3. Place the rice paper wrappers in a heatproof bowl and cover with hot water, then leave to soak for 5 minutes, until soft and pliable. (Or prepare according to packet instructions.)

4. Drain the wrappers on a clean tea towel and lay a few coriander leaves along the middle of each one. Add a few leaves of Vietnamese hot mint and sweet Thai basil. Arrange 3 prawns on each one and then scatter over the cucumber, carrot and spring onions. Make sure you don't over-fill the papers as they may split if you do.

5. Fold the side of each rice paper in, then roll up to make a neat cylindrical shape. Just before serving mix the coriander and mint into the dipping sauce and serve immediately.

Serves 4

36 cooked tiger prawns, peeled
12 rice paper wrappers (each about 7.5 x 15cm) or iceberg lettuce leaves
Handful of coriander leaves
Handful of Vietnamese hot mint leaves
Handful of sweet Thai basil
1 cucumber, julienned
1 carrot, julienned
2 spring onions, julienned

For the Vietnamese dipping sauce (nuoc cham)
3 tbsp lime juice
1 tbsp caster sugar
2½ tbsp fish sauce (nam pla)
1 small garlic clove, finely minced
1–2 small Thai chillies, thinly sliced
Handful of coriander leaves, finely chopped
Handful of Vietnamese hot mint leaves, finely chopped

Sushi Salmon and Avocado Miso Rice Bowl

This is a deconstructed sushi roll that saves you all the painstaking rolling and shaping but retains all the goodness. I've decided to use brown sushi rice but any short grain brown rice will work perfectly well – simply follow the instructions on the packet. If you don't want to go to the bother of curing your own salmon simply use a good-quality smoked salmon.

Serves 4

200g brown sushi rice
1 ripe avocado, peeled, stoned and thinly sliced
Large handful of wild rocket leaves
1 nori sheet, sliced into thin strips

For the salmon
2 tsp Sichuan peppercorns
2 tsp coriander seeds
3 tbsp sea salt flakes or rock salt
2 tbsp sugar
500g organic salmon fillet (from the thick end), pin-boned, skinned and all dark flesh removed

For the miso dressing
1 tsp English mustard
1 tsp light miso paste
2 tsp rice vinegar
1 tsp light soy sauce
3 tbsp rapeseed oil
2 tsp toasted sesame oil

1. To prepare the salmon, grind the peppercorns and coriander seeds to a coarse texture in a spice grinder or with a pestle and mortar. Mix the peppercorn mixture with the salt and sugar and tip onto a large plate. Roll the salmon in the mixture until it is evenly coated. Wrap it really well with cling film and leave in the fridge for 2–3 hours. The cure will have drawn out some of the liquid from the fish and the flesh should feel firmer. If you are making this more than 3 hours in advance, wipe off the cure at this point (do not rinse) then re-wrap in cling film and keep in the fridge until ready to use.

2. Place the rice in a pan and cover with cold water, then leave to soak for 30 minutes. Strain through a sieve and then return to the pan. Fill with boiling water so that the rice is covered with about 5cm of water. Cover with a tight-fitting lid and simmer for 30–40 minutes, until all of the water has been absorbed.

3. To make the dressing, put the mustard and miso in a bowl with the vinegar and soy sauce and mix well. Slowly drizzle in the rapeseed oil and the sesame oil until you have a smooth emulsion.

4. To serve, divide the brown sushi rice among 4 deep bowls. Wipe the excess cure off the salmon and cut into 5mm-thick slices (always cut against the grain). Arrange the sliced salmon on top of the rice with slices of avocado and a small mound of rocket. Drizzle the miso dressing on top and scatter over the nori strips to serve.

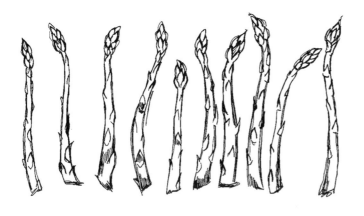

quick
cook
suppers

While I like to spend time in the kitchen, more often than not I end up racing home, hungry and ready to eat. Recipes for quick cook suppers are essential, especially when you are trying to eat lighter, fresher and healthier meals. I think it has to be one of the trickiest times of day to choose something good for you. The real dilemma is coming home to an empty kitchen with little to work with, so it really comes down to planning and making sure that you have the basics that you can rely on to make something quick and nourishing.

Recipes with big, bold flavours never fail to excite me and there are plenty to choose from here for your quick-cooking supper of choice! Whether it's vibrant salads you're after, like Tequila Chicken Quinoa Mango Salad, with crunch from nuts and the freshness of herbs like coriander and mint, or the deep, dark comfort and spice from something like the delicious Harissa Baked Eggs, having recipes like these to rely on is essential to your fresh and lighter eating repertoire. And dinner options like Coriander and Sesame Fishcakes with Spiralized Thai Salad, Tiger's Milk Sea Bass Ceviche with Quinoa Salad or Healthy Nasi Goreng are bound to excite the taste buds in a hurry!

Having your store cupboard well stocked with grains, pulses, noodles, sauces and spices really comes into play when cooking at speed. Having these types of ingredients to hand means you don't have to break the bank every time you hit the shops – all that's required is fresh vegetables, meat, chicken or fish. This sort of forward thinking and planning makes it a whole lot easier to make good food decisions.

Basically a pimped-up fried rice, Nasi Goreng is the staple diet of backpackers and locals in Indonesia and Malaysia. Cheap to make, full of flavour and topped with a fried egg – what's not to like? I've given it a healthy twist by unashamedly using uber trendy cauliflower rice, which is high in vitamin C, but you could also make it with quinoa or brown rice. The backbone of the recipe begins with a vibrant paste humming with sweet and electric flavours.

Healthy Nasi Goreng

1. Devein the prawns if necessary: if there is a black line down the back of the prawn use a small, sharp knife to make a shallow cut along the length of the line and carefully lift it out using the tip of the knife.

2. To make cauliflower rice, place the florets in a food processor. Blitz until you have a fine consistency, almost like fluffed-up couscous. Set aside.

3. Blitz all the ingredients for the paste in a food processor until you have a smooth mixture. In a large wok or deep frying pan, heat 1 teaspoon of the sunflower oil over a high heat. Add half of the paste and stir-fry for 1 minute, until sizzling and aromatic.

4. Add the carrot and spring onions and stir-fry for 3 minutes, until just cooked through. Add the prawns and peas and stir-fry until the prawns are no longer translucent. Transfer to a bowl and keep warm.

5. In the same pan, heat another teaspoon of oil, if required, and fry the remaining paste as before. Add the cauliflower rice, soy sauce and kecap manis and fry for 3–4 minutes, or until the cauliflower rice is coated and piping hot. Return the vegetables and prawns to the wok and toss well until hot all the way through.

6. Divide the Nasi Goreng between 4 plates and set aside while you quickly fry the eggs in the remaining oil in a clean frying pan. Serve each plateful topped with a fried egg, a sprinkling of sliced spring onions and chilli. Add some prawn crackers if you fancy going to town!

Serves 4

300g raw king prawns, peeled
3 tsp sunflower oil
1 carrot, finely chopped
2 spring onions, sliced, plus extra to serve
100g frozen peas
1 large head cauliflower, broken into florets
1 tbsp dark soy sauce
1 tbsp kecap manis (Indonesian sweet soy sauce)
4 large eggs
1 red chilli, sliced, to serve
Prawn crackers, to serve (optional)

For the paste
1 tbsp groundnut oil
4 garlic cloves
2 red chillies
Thumb-sized piece of fresh ginger, peeled and roughly chopped
1 tbsp toasted mixed seeds
1 tsp ground turmeric
1 tsp coriander seeds
Zest and juice of 1 lime
1 tbsp fish sauce (nam pla)
1 tbsp tomato ketchup
2 large shallots, peeled and roughly chopped

Harissa Baked Eggs

Whether for brunch, lunch or dinner, these baked eggs are a speedy way to provide booming flavour and a dose of healthy comfort food. A basic tomato sauce is the hallmark of any good home cook and here it is put to good use to coddle eggs until their yolks are runny and dreamy. With an injection of dark heat from the harissa paste, for me this is all too often the answer to the question: 'What's for dinner?'

Serves 4

1 tbsp olive oil
1 large onion, very finely diced
2 garlic cloves, very finely chopped
1 red chilli, finely diced
1 tsp smoked paprika
3–4 heaped tbsp harissa paste
2 x 400g tins plum tomatoes
Large handful of coriander, roughly chopped
4 large free-range eggs
Sea salt and freshly ground black pepper
Toasted Super Seed Bread slices (see page 202), to serve

1. Heat the olive oil in a high-sided, ovenproof frying pan over a medium heat and fry the onion for 6–8 minutes, or until softened. Add the garlic, chilli and paprika and fry for 1–2 minutes, or until the mixture becomes aromatic.

2. Stir in the harissa paste and tomatoes, pressing the tomatoes down with the back of a fork until you are left with a smooth-ish consistency. Cook for 8–10 minutes at a gentle simmer, until the sauce thickens and intensifies. Season to taste. Preheat the oven to 200°C (180°C fan).

3. Stir through the coriander, reserving a few leaves to garnish. If you want an even smoother sauce, transfer to a food processor and blitz until velvety and then return to the pan (or use individual ovenproof dishes).

4. Use the back of a ladle to make 4 wells in the sauce and crack an egg into each one. Bake in the oven for 10 minutes, until the eggs are just set but the yolks are still runny. Scatter over the reserved coriander leaves and devour with warm toasted slices of Super Seed Bread for dipping.

Tiger's Milk Sea Bass Ceviche with Quinoa Salad

The idea of fish marinated in fruit juice might seem like an odd combination but ceviche is having a moment, and rightly so. A fresh and vibrant traditional recipe from South America, it relies on the acidity of lime to cure the fish and infuse it with intense flavour. With only a handful of ingredients, the results are fairly impressive.

Serves 4

600g sea bass fillets, skinned and pin-boned
2 green chillies, finely chopped
Juice of 3 limes
Juice of 1 orange
½ red onion, finely sliced
Large handful of coriander, roughly chopped
Sea salt

For the quinoa salad
200g quinoa
Juice of 1 lime
1 cucumber, deseeded and sliced in half moons
250g cherry tomatoes, diced
1 avocado, roughly diced
Large handful of mint leaves, roughly chopped
Large handful of coriander, roughly chopped

1. Slice the fish into 2cm cubes, place in a bowl and season with sea salt. Let sit for 2–3 minutes before adding the chillies, lime and orange juices. Leave to marinate in the fridge for 10 minutes. Add the red onion and coriander to the bowl and toss to combine.

2. Cook the quinoa (see page 214) and then spread out on a shallow dish to cool. When cool squeeze over the lime juice and mix through the remaining salad ingredients. Season with sea salt to taste.

3. Serve the ceviche in individual portions with the quinoa salad on the side.

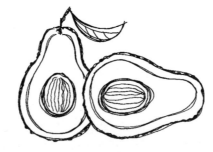

Yakitori Salmon Skewers with Red Rice Salad

The Japanese dish yakitori generally refers to skewers of chicken, grilled over charcoal to give a unique smoky taste. They are often enjoyed as a street food snack with a cold beer; here I have given them a small makeover using salmon and serving them with a vibrant red rice salad. If you can't get your hands on red rice, use brown rice instead.

Serves 4

2 tbsp dark soy sauce
1 tbsp sake
1 tbsp mirin
1tsp dark brown sugar
500g skinless salmon fillet, cut in 3cm cubes
6 shiitake mushrooms, stem removed and cut into 1cm slices
5 spring onions, cut in 3cm pieces
1 tbsp sesame seeds, toasted

For the warm red rice salad
250g red rice
1 tbsp miso paste
1 tbsp mirin
1 tbsp rice vinegar
1 tsp clear honey
200g kale leaves, torn from stem and roughly chopped
2 carrots, shaved into ribbons
½ cucumber, shaved into ribbons
2 nori sheets, sliced into strips

1. In a bowl whisk together the soy sauce, sake, mirin and brown sugar until the sugar has dissolved. Add the salmon pieces and toss to combine. Cover and chill in the fridge for about 30 minutes.

2. Thread the salmon cubes, shiitake mushrooms and spring onions onto wooden or bamboo skewers (you should get about 2 skewers per person). Cover and chill in the fridge for 15 minutes, or until you are ready to cook.

3. For the red rice salad, cook the rice until tender according to the packet instructions. Drain and rinse under cold water.

4. In a large bowl whisk together the miso paste, mirin, rice vinegar and honey. Add the kale and massage until tender. Add the carrot and cucumber ribbons, cooked rice and nori strips.

5. When you're ready to cook the skewers, place a griddle pan over a high heat and cook each skewer for about 2–3 minutes each side. Brush with any remaining marinade as they cook.

6. Sprinkle the sesame seeds over the skewers and serve with bowls of the red rice salad.

Coriander and Sesame Fishcakes with Spiralized Thai Salad

I have yet to travel to a city with more fascinating food markets than Bangkok. They can be daunting to a Western traveller at first, but there is nothing like being shovelled along by locals who know where to seek the best ingredients, and discovering that every stallholder offers something more intriguing than the next. These vibrant fishcakes are inspired by those markets and while a spiralized salad might not be found at many Thai street food stalls, this clever little kitchen gadget is put to good use to make a crunchy salad with a classic Thai dressing.

Serves 4

450g skinless white fish fillets, such as haddock or cod, cut into large chunks
1 tbsp fish sauce (nam pla)
1 large egg
1 tbsp red curry paste
1 red chilli, roughly chopped
2 garlic cloves
Thumb-sized piece of fresh ginger, peeled and roughly chopped
Large handful of fresh coriander, stalks and leaves, roughly chopped
Zest and juice of 1 lime
3–4 spring onions, finely sliced
3 tbsp sesame seeds
2 tbsp coconut oil
Sweet chilli dipping sauce, to serve

For the salad
1 tsp caster sugar
Zest and juice of 1 lime
3 tbsp fish sauce (nom pla)
1 red chilli, finely chopped
Large handful of peanuts, toasted
1 carrot, spiralized or julienned
1 cucumber, spiralized or julienned
3–4 spring onions, finely sliced
Large handful of mint leaves, roughly chopped

1. Place the fish in a food processor and blitz for 3 seconds or so until smooth. Add the fish sauce, egg, curry paste, chilli, garlic, ginger, coriander stalks and lime zest and juice and blitz again until everything is combined and the mixture begins to ball together and become thicker. Remove the blade from the food processor and stir through the coriander leaves and spring onions.

2. With damp hands, form the mixture into 12 balls and flatten to make fishcakes. Roll each one in the sesame seeds to coat.

3. Heat the coconut oil in a large frying pan over a medium heat and fry the fishcakes in two batches for about 2–3 minutes on each side. Remove with a fish slice and drain on a plate lined with kitchen paper.

4. Whisk together the caster sugar, lime zest and juice, fish sauce and chilli in a large bowl until the caster sugar has dissolved. Bash the peanuts roughly in a pestle and mortar.

5. Add the carrot, cucumber, spring onions and mint leaves to the dressing. Toss everything together until the salad is completely coated in the dressing. Stir through the bashed peanuts, reserving about a tablespoon.

6. Serve the salad topped with the fishcakes. Drizzle with sweet chilli sauce and scatter over the reserved peanuts.

Pan-fried Cod with Minty Pea Purée

I love the simplicity of pan-fried fish – it's the ultimate fast food. Served with the clean flavours of pea and mint and bulked out with Puy lentils, this makes a snappy supper from very few ingredients.

Serves 4

4 tbsp extra-virgin olive oil
1 shallot, finely chopped
450g frozen peas
Small handful of mint leaves, finely chopped
1 garlic clove, finely chopped
Large handful of flat-leaf parsley leaves, finely chopped
4 cod fillets (about 150g each), skin on
200g tinned Puy lentils, drained and rinsed
Zest and juice of 1 lemon
Sea salt and freshly ground black pepper
4 tbsp natural yoghurt, to serve

1. Heat 1 teaspoon of the olive oil in a frying pan over a medium-high heat, add the shallot and fry for 2–3 minutes, or until softened. Add the peas to the pan with 50ml of water and simmer for 5 minutes until the peas are just tender. Drain away any excess liquid and then tip the contents of the pan into the bowl of a food processor. Add the mint leaves and blitz until completely smooth. Season to taste.

2. In a small bowl whisk together 3 tablespoons of the olive oil with the garlic and parsley. Season the cod fillets with salt and pepper.

3. Heat the remaining olive oil in a large frying pan over a medium-high heat and fry the cod, skin side down, for 4–5 minutes, depending on the thickness of the fillets. Carefully turn over and continue to cook for 1–2 minutes, or until just cooked through (the flesh should be just opaque).

4. Warm the lentils through in a pan and mix in the lemon zest and juice and all but a tablespoon of the parsley oil.

5. Spread the pea purée on serving plates, top with the lentils and place a cod fillet on top. Add a dollop of yoghurt to each cod fillet and drizzle with the remaining parsley oil. Serve immediately.

Pea, Asparagus and Ricotta Frittata

Simple greens wrapped up with creamy ricotta and just-set eggs are one of the quickest suppers to make. This is a dish that is also impressive-looking enough to serve straight to the table as a dinner party starter.

Serves 4

Small bunch of asparagus, ends trimmed
6 spring onions, trimmed
8 large free-range eggs
60ml goats' milk
Small handful of basil, roughly chopped, plus a few leaves to garnish
Zest of 1 lemon
150g frozen peas, defrosted
1 tsp olive oil
100g ricotta cheese
Sea salt and freshly ground black pepper

1. Preheat the grill to medium-high.

2. Blanch the asparagus and spring onions for 1–2 minutes in a pan of boiling salted water. Drain and refresh in a bowl of ice-cold water.

3. In a bowl, whisk the eggs and milk together then season and stir through the basil, lemon zest and peas.

4. Heat the olive oil in a large nonstick frying pan and pour in the egg mixture. Working quickly, arrange the asparagus and spring onions over the top of the frittata and dot with teaspoons of ricotta. Cook gently until the mixture is set but still a little runny in the centre. Place the pan under the hot grill and cook until the egg on top is golden and bubbling.

5. Serve in big chunky quarters with a scattering of basil leaves.

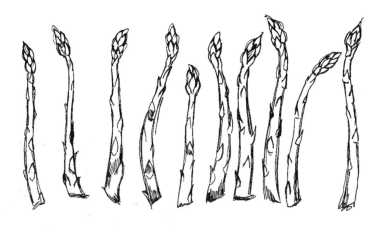

It may feel like a cheat using a curry paste, but if you can find a good-quality one that you like the taste of, it can be the key to one of the quickest suppers you will make. With firm pieces of fish, tender sweet potato, sweet cherry tomatoes and crunchy sugar snap peas all wrapped up in a creamy spicy broth, this makes a hearty and nutritious supper, especially when served with quinoa.

Thai Red Curry

1. While the quinoa is cooking, heat the oil in a separate large pan over a medium-high heat and add the shallots and ginger. Fry for 3–4 minutes until softened. Add the curry paste, tomatoes and sweet potato and stir-fry for a further 2–3 minutes.

2. Pour in the coconut milk and vegetable stock, bring to the boil and then reduce the heat to a steady simmer and cook for 10–12 minutes, or until the sweet potato is tender. Add the fish sauce, brown sugar, sugar snap peas and baby corn and simmer for 3 minutes. Squeeze in the lime juice, stir through and taste, adjusting with more fish sauce, sugar or lime juice if you think it needs it.

3. Add the fish pieces and simmer for 3–5 minutes until just cooked. Stir through some of the basil and coriander leaves before serving over bowls of quinoa. Garnish with the remaining basil and coriander leaves.

Serves 4

250g cooked quinoa (see page 214)
1 tbsp rapeseed oil
2 shallots, peeled and finely sliced
Thumb-sized piece of fresh ginger, peeled and finely sliced
3 tbsp Thai red curry paste
150g cherry tomatoes
1 large sweet potato, peeled and diced
1 x 400ml light coconut milk
200ml vegetable stock
1 tbsp Thai fish sauce (nam pla)
1 tsp brown sugar
150g sugar snap peas
190g baby corn
Juice of 2 limes
600g skinless fish fillet, such as cod or haddock, cut into 2.5cm cubes
Small handful each of basil and coriander leaves, roughly torn

The meaty flavour of mushrooms lends itself extremely well to this 'orzotto' using pearl barley, a hearty, nutty flavoured grain. To intensify the flavour of this dish, soak some dried porcini mushrooms in boiling water for a few minutes and add to the risotto along with their soaking liquid.

Pearl Barley and Mushroom Risotto

1. Place the dried mushrooms in a bowl and cover with hot water. Allow to soak for 5–10 minutes.

2. Heat 1 teaspoon of the olive oil in a large non-stick frying pan over a medium-high heat and add the mixed mushrooms. Fry until just tender then stir through the garlic and season to taste. Fry for a further two minutes before removing from the heat. Stir through the parsley, reserving a little to garnish. Drain the dried mushrooms, reserving the soaking liquid for later, and stir them into the pan. Transfer the mushroom mixture to a plate and set aside.

3. Heat the remaining oil in the same pan over a medium high heat and sauté the shallots gently for 8 minutes, or until they become soft and sweet. Stir through the thyme and pearl barley and fry gently before adding the wine and cooking for 2 minutes to allow the grains to soak up the flavours in the pan. Pour in just enough stock to cover the pearl barley and then allow to bubble away until all the liquid has been absorbed. Repeat this process, adding the stock a little at a time, until the barley is tender and has absorbed all the liquid (this should take about 35 minutes).

4. Stir through the pecorino and mushrooms. Taste and adjust the seasoning. If the risotto is too dry, add a splash of boiling water. Serve the risotto in shallow bowls with a sprinkling of parsley, a drizzle of extra-virgin olive oil and some more grated pecorino.

Serves 4

25g dried mushrooms
3 tbsp olive oil
350g mixed mushrooms
2 garlic cloves, finely chopped
Large handful of flat-leaf parsley, roughly chopped
3 shallots, finely chopped
3 thyme sprigs, leaves finely chopped
300g pearl barley
75ml white wine
1 litre vegetable stock
50g grated pecorino, plus extra to serve
Sea salt and freshly ground black pepper
Extra-virgin olive oil, to serve

Tequila Chicken Quinoa Mango Salad

I'm a bit of a lightweight when it comes to booze as my friends like to remind me on a constant basis. I'd sooner use tequila in cooking than down a shot of the stuff as in this recipe, where the tequila lends a peppery sharpness to the lime- and mint-infused chicken marinade, which will give you extra tender meat. Paired with a sweet and savoury mango quinoa salad, it may almost make you forget your late night misadventures… well, almost.

Serves 4

For the chicken
4 skinless chicken breasts (about 150g each)
1 garlic clove
1 green chilli
6 tbsp tequila
Zest and juice of 2 limes
1 tsp chilli powder
1 tbsp olive oil
Small handful of fresh mint leaves, chopped
Generous pinch of sea salt and freshly ground pepper
olive oil, for brushing

For the mango salad
1 tsp caster sugar
Juice of 1 lime
3 tbsp fish sauce (nam pla)
200g cooked quinoa (see page 214)
150g beansprouts
5 spring onions, thinly sliced
1 ripe mango, peeled, stoned and sliced lengthways
2 Little Gem lettuces, roughly shredded
Handful of peanuts, toasted and chopped
Handful of fresh mint, chopped
Handful of fresh coriander, chopped

1. Place all the ingredients for the chicken into a resealable bag and shake to combine. Leave to marinate in the fridge for at least 2 hours, ideally overnight, turning once or twice if you remember.

2. Whisk together the caster sugar, lime juice and fish sauce in a large bowl until the sugar has completely dissolved. Add the quinoa, beansprouts, spring onions, mango and the torn lettuce and toss to combine.

3. Place a large griddle pan over a medium-high heat and brush lightly with oil. Remove the chicken breasts from the marinade and fry for 4–5 minutes on each side, or until cooked all the way through. Remove from the heat and slice each breast into chunks.

4. Divide the mango quinoa salad between 4 plates and sprinkle each one with some chopped peanuts, mint and coriander. Top with the chicken slices and serve immediately.

One of my favourite Thai salads is this minced chicken one (laab gai), which is full of fresh flavour from the mint leaves and lime juice. It can also be made with pork mince or a vegetarian mince alternative.

Thai Minced Chicken Salad

1. Toast the rice in a large dry frying pan over a medium-high heat, until golden brown. Transfer to a pestle and mortar and pound the rice – you are looking for a rough texture rather than a fine powder. Set aside.

2. Place the garlic, chilli and ginger in a food processor and whizz until finely chopped. Add the chicken and pulse until smooth.

3. Heat the sunflower oil in the same frying pan over a high heat, add the minced chicken and fry for 2–3 minutes, breaking the chicken up with a spatula as it cooks. Continue to cook until the chicken is cooked all the way through, browns slightly and is broken into small pieces.

4. Add the fish sauce and sugar and stir through, frying for another minute until you have a good colour on the meat. Add half the spring onions, the mint, toasted rice and lime juice and zest and fry for 1–2 minutes, until the spring onions are just tender.

5. Arrange the lettuce leaves on two plates and top with the chicken mixture. Garnish with extra mint leaves and remaining spring onions. Serve warm.

Serves 2

50g Thai sticky rice
3 garlic cloves, finely chopped
1 red chilli, deseeded and finely chopped
Thumb-sized piece of fresh ginger, peeled
1 tbsp sunflower oil
2 large, skinless chicken breasts (about 150g each), cut into large chunks
1 tbsp fish sauce (nam pla)
1 tsp caster sugar
5 spring onions, finely chopped
Generous handful of fresh mint leaves, roughly chopped
Zest and juice of 1 lime
2 Little Gem lettuces, leaves separated

Nutty Chicken Satay Salad

As crunchy, creamy, nutty chicken satay salads go, this one has a lot to offer. Based on one of my favourite Asian street foods, chicken satay, it's got all the best bits – tender chicken in an aromatic peanut sauce along with a simple crunchy salad. Mix and match the vegetables listed here as you wish but do choose ones that have a bite to them.

Serves 4

2 large, skinless chicken breasts (about 150g each), thinly sliced
1 tbsp turmeric
2 tsp ground coriander
1 tsp ground cumin
2 garlic cloves, finely chopped
Thumb-sized piece of fresh ginger, finely chopped
1 tsp sugar
1 tsp rapeseed oil
1 courgette
1 cucumber
2 large carrots
5 spring onions, finely sliced on the diagonal
Handful of salted peanuts, roughly chopped

For the peanut satay sauce
1 tsp sunflower oil
1 garlic clove, very finely chopped
Small thumb-sized piece of fresh ginger, peeled and very finely chopped
1 small red chilli, deseeded and finely chopped
200ml light coconut milk
Juice of 1 lime
3 tbsp crunchy peanut butter
½ tbsp dark soy sauce

1. Place the sliced chicken in a large bowl with the turmeric, coriander, cumin, garlic, ginger and sugar and toss to coat. Leave to marinate for 30 minutes, ideally overnight if you have time.

2. Heat the rapeseed oil in a large frying pan over a medium high heat. Fry the chicken for 6–8 minutes, or until cooked all the way through.

3. To make the peanut sauce, heat the oil in a small pan, add the garlic, ginger and chilli and fry for 30–40 seconds, stirring continuously. Add the coconut milk, lime juice, peanut butter and soy sauce. Bring to the boil, stirring to melt the peanut butter, then reduce the heat and simmer for 2–3 minutes.

4. Use a julienne peeler or spiralizer to make long strands of the courgette, cucumber and carrots. Place the raw veggie noodles in a large mixing bowl and add most of the spring onions, saving a few to use as a garnish. Pour in the peanut sauce and toss all the ingredients together until combined. Serve with the chicken pieces and a sprinkle of chopped peanuts and the reserved spring onion slices. Enjoy warm or cold in a takeaway lunch box.

Poached Coconut Chicken

A delicate and light chicken dish that is full of exotic flavours. The fresh bite and crunch from the vegetables in the rich coconut sauce works really well.

Serves 2

Zest and juice of 2 limes
Small thumb-sized piece of fresh ginger, peeled and chopped
Large handful of coriander leaves and stalks, roughly chopped
2 lemongrass stalks, trimmed and roughly chopped
1 tsp rapeseed oil
1 x 400ml tin light coconut milk
2 large skinless chicken breast fillets (about 150g each), cut into strips
3 tbsp Thai fish sauce (nam pla)
1 tsp sesame oil
225g Thai flat rice noodles, cooked
2 bok choy, roughly sliced
1 cucumber, shaved into ribbons (using a vegetable peeler)
2 celery sticks, thinly sliced
1 bunch spring onions, trimmed and thinly sliced on the diagonal

1. Use a hand-held stick blender or mini food processor to blitz the lime zest, ginger, coriander stalks and lemongrass until you have a smooth paste.

2. Heat the rapeseed oil in a large wok over a high heat. Add the paste and fry for 1–2 minutes until it is aromatic. Add the coconut milk and mix through, then stir in the chicken strips and allow to cook on a gentle heat for 8 minutes. Add the fish sauce and simmer for another 5 minutes. Add the lime juice and sesame oil and stir through. Remove the chicken and slice into bite-sized pieces.

3. Warm the cooked noodles by covering them with boiling water. Drain and divide between 2 shallow bowls, then top with the bok choy, cucumber, celery and chicken pieces. Ladle over the hot coconut broth and garnish with sliced spring onions and coriander leaves.

Chicken Schnitzel with Little Gem and Pea Caesar

A perfectly cooked chicken schnitzel is a beautiful thing, particularly when it is served with my simplified version of a Caesar salad. I like to make this with the first of my own home-grown garden peas, which are so sweet they can be eaten raw.

Serves 2

2 large skinless chicken breast fillets (about 150g each)
100g rustic breadcrumbs (preferably sourdough)
3 tbsp freshly grated Parmesan
1 tbsp freshly chopped flat-leaf parsley
1 egg
2 tbsp milk
25g seasoned flour
3 tbsp rapeseed oil
4 Little Gem lettuces, trimmed and quartered
50g freshly podded peas

For the Caesar dressing
1 medium egg
2 anchovy fillets (from a jar or tin)
Few drops of Worcestershire sauce
1 tsp lemon juice
120ml rapeseed oil
Sea salt and freshly ground black pepper

1. First make the Caesar dressing. Put the egg, anchovy fillets, Worcestershire sauce and lemon juice in a mini food processor and process until just combined. With the motor running, gradually add the rapeseed oil and process until thick and creamy. Season with salt and pepper and add a little water if you find the dressing a little thick.

2. Slice each chicken fillet in half and then flatten the pieces slightly by placing between 2 sheets of clingfilm and bashing with a rolling pin to make thin escalopes. Place the breadcrumbs in a bowl with the Parmesan and parsley and beat the egg and milk together in a separate bowl. Dust the chicken escalopes in the seasoned flour, then dip in the beaten egg mixture and coat in the breadcrumbs.

3. Place a large, non-stick frying pan over a medium-high heat. When the pan is hot add the rapeseed oil and then add the coated chicken escalopes. Cook for 2–3 minutes on each side, turning once, until the chicken is cooked through and the Parmesan crumbs are golden. Drain on kitchen paper.

4. Arrange the Little Gem lettuces, cut sides up, on each plate and scatter over the peas. Drizzle the Caesar dressing over the salad, and then add a chicken schnitzel to each plate to serve.

time
for
dinner

Time to get down to business! Fresh and light dinners require some new thinking, an injection of vegetables, some exciting cooking methods, a little less meat and, when you do cook with it, meat of higher quality. My main aim with lighter meals is to not compromise on the flavour; instead I put it at the forefront of each dish. In these recipes I rely on cooking methods like roasting, which brings out the natural sweetness of vegetables, zingy and tangy dressings and salsas to add a final punch to dishes, electric spice mixes to take fish, chicken, grains and more to another level and – rather importantly – a focus on contrasting textures: crunch and silkiness, crisp and chewiness. All these elements are bound to excite the palate.

There are quite a few vegetable-centric recipes here for healthier evening meals which don't skimp on the flavour front, dishes like Roast Squash Salad with Sriracha Yoghurt and Coriander Salsa, Mediterranean Vegetable Tart (with a slightly controversial goat's cheese cauliflower crust, which is surprisingly brilliant!), a completely meat-free Super Power Chilli with Charred Corn Salsa with all the extra elements you would come to expect and the brilliant blushing Mega Beetroot Burgers, which look nearly as good as they taste! On the non-vegetarian front there are also dishes to delight like Spiced Fish with Mango Salsa and Brown Rice Salad or Pomegranate Molasses Chicken, my new way to roast chicken, served with roasted vegetables that have been tossed through bulgur wheat – an all-in-one dish that is perfect for serving to the table. There are also four great side dishes to choose from, all of which would happily sit alongside many of the recipes in this chapter. However, I can also never speak highly enough of the humble salad: a bowl of simply dressed leaves is always a welcome addition and will boost your intake of greens.

Roast Chickpea, Carrot, Mint and Halloumi Salad

I am slightly addicted to halloumi cheese; its saltiness and unique texture and the fact that it can be fried makes it a great alternative to meat in a salad like this. Roasting chickpeas gives them an altogether different texture, slightly crispy on the outside, making them perfect for adding to salads or just as a simple snack.

Serves 4

1 x 400g tin chickpeas, drained and rinsed
300g cherry tomatoes, halved
2 tsp rapeseed oil, plus extra for frying
1 tsp smoked paprika
200g halloumi cheese, cut into 1cm thick slices
1 Little Gem lettuce, leaves separated
2 large carrots, cut into julienne strips
½ red onion, thinly sliced
Sea salt and freshly ground black pepper

For the dressing
3 tbsp extra-virgin olive oil
1 tbsp lemon juice
1 tbsp cider vinegar
1 tsp Dijon mustard
1 garlic clove, very finely chopped

1. Preheat the oven to 200°C (180°C fan).

2. Place the chickpeas and tomatoes in a roasting tin and drizzle over the oil. Season with salt and pepper and sprinkle over the paprika; toss to coat. Roast in the oven for about 35 minutes, or until the tomatoes have shrunk and become caramelised.

3. Whisk together all the ingredients for the dressing in a large mixing bowl and set aside.

4. Heat a little rapeseed oil in a large frying pan over a medium-high heat and add the halloumi slices. Season with salt and pepper while they are in the pan and fry on both sides until they are golden brown. Remove from the pan and set aside.

5. Add the Little Gem leaves, carrot, red onion, tomatoes and chickpeas to the bowl of dressing and mix until all the ingredients are coated.

6. Pile the salad onto plates and top with the slices of halloumi.

Pumpkins and squash are two of my favourite vegetables to grow. There are so many incredible varieties, shapes and sizes and I love the way they grow with vigour through the summer months, from floppy golden flowers into tough orbs ready for the autumn. Roasting them brings out their sweetness and makes them a meaty main ingredient that's ideal for a salad of sorts like this one, laced with a vibrant and sharp aromatic coriander salsa.

Roast Squash Salad with Sriracha Yoghurt

1. Preheat the oven to 200°C (180°C fan).

2. Place the squash and red onion quarters into a large roasting tin and drizzle with oil. Sprinkle over the cumin, chilli flakes and smoked paprika and mix until completely coated. Roast in the oven for 45 minutes, or until the squash is tender and slightly caramelised.

3. For the salsa, whizz the oil, coriander, chilli and lime zest and juice together in a food processor until completely combined. Set aside. Prepare the sriracha yoghurt by stirring together the yoghurt and hot sauce. Season with salt and pepper and set aside.

4. Mix together the fennel, lentils and chickpeas in a large bowl and then stir in half the coriander salsa.

5. Divide the fennel, lentil and chickpea mixture between 4 plates and top with the roasted squash and onions. Add a dollop of sriracha yoghurt and the remaining coriander salsa. Finally sprinkle with toasted seeds and scatter with coriander leaves.

Serves 4

2 small butternut squash, peeled and cut into wedges
2 small red onions, quartered with the root left intact
1 tbsp rapeseed oil
1 tsp ground cumin
1 tsp red chilli flakes
1 tsp smoked paprika
2 fennel bulbs, thinly sliced
1 x 400g tin Puy lentils, drained and rinsed
1 x 400g tin chickpeas, drained and rinsed

For the coriander salsa
2 tbsp extra-virgin olive oil
Large handful of coriander, plus extra to garnish
1 green chilli, finely chopped
Zest and juice of 1 lime
Sea salt

For the Sriracha Yoghurt
6 tbsp natural yoghurt
1 tsp sriracha hot sauce
Sea salt and freshly ground black pepper

Squash, Spinach and Chickpea Filo Pie

This filo pie would make a fantastic vegetarian centrepiece at a dinner party but it would also be delicious taken warm from the oven on a picnic. Remember to cover the unused sheets of filo with a damp tea towel as you work to prevent them drying out.

Serves 6

4 tbsp rapeseed oil
1 small onion, diced
1 large garlic clove, finely chopped
1 heaped tsp grated fresh ginger
1 tsp garam masala
½ tsp each of ground cumin and coriander
450g sweet potatoes, peeled and diced
1 x 400g tin chickpeas, drained and rinsed
200ml vegetable stock
1 x 400g tin chopped tomatoes
125ml light coconut milk
Good pinch of sugar (optional)
100g frozen spinach
8–10 filo pastry sheets, thawed if frozen
Sea salt and freshly ground black pepper
Lightly dressed mixed green salad, to serve

1. Heat 1 tablespoon of the rapeseed oil in a large, heavy-based pan and sauté the onion, until softened and just beginning to colour around the edges. Stir in the garlic and ginger and cook for another 30 seconds or so. Add the spices and cook for a further minute, stirring.

2. Tip the sweet potatoes and chickpeas into the pan and mix well to combine, then allow to sauté for a couple of minutes. Stir in the stock, tomatoes, coconut milk and sugar, if using. Season with salt and pepper. Bring to the boil, then reduce the heat and simmer for about 15 minutes, or until the sweet potatoes are completely tender but still holding their shape.

3. Fold the spinach into the sweet potato mixture and cook for another couple of minutes until the spinach is cooked through and tender. The mixture should be nice and chunky at this point – any excess liquid should be reduced down. Remove from the heat and leave to cool completely.

4. Preheat the oven to 180°C (160°C fan). Brush the base and sides of a large 1.5-litre ovenproof frying pan with rapeseed oil (or you can use a 23cm loose-bottomed cake tin).

5. Brush 4–6 of the filo sheets with rapeseed oil, then lay them in the base of the pan or tin so they drape over the sides. Spoon in the cooled sweet potato mixture and spread out over the base. Fold the overhanging pastry over to cover the filling. Scrunch the remaining filo sheets and arrange on top to cover the top of the pie (you may not need all of them), brushing with a little extra oil. Bake for 25–30 minutes, or until the filo is crisp and golden.

6. If using a frying pan, carefully slide the pie on to a board (or remove it from the tin). Serve cut into slices with green salad.

Squash Tagine with Quinoa

Although I do own a traditional tagine, it rarely makes an appearance when I cook this dish as I tend to use a deep-sided frying pan, which does the job perfectly. Instead my poor conical tagine is relegated to the bottom shelf of my cupboard where it sits being judged by all the regular kitchenware, jealous of their ability to stack correctly. Whatever you choose to cook this recipe in, you are in for a treat. It's a stunning medley of sweet, vitamin-packed vegetables in a subtly spiced tomato sauce bursting with jewels of dried fruit.

Serves 4

50g dried apricots, finely sliced
50g sultanas
1 tsp ground ginger
1 tsp freshly ground black pepper
1 tsp ground turmeric
1 tsp cayenne pepper
2 tsp smoked paprika
1 tbsp rapeseed oil
2 onions, roughly chopped
8 garlic cloves, finely chopped
1 butternut squash, peeled and cut into bite-sized pieces
2 large carrots, cut into bite-sized pieces
1 courgette, cut into bite-sized pieces
1 tbsp honey
2 x 400g tins chopped tomatoes
½ tbsp vegetable bouillon powder
1 x 400g tin chickpeas, drained and rinsed
250g quinoa
Handful of toasted flaked almonds, plus extra to serve
Handful of fresh coriander, roughly chopped, plus extra to serve

1. Place the apricots and sultanas in small bowl and pour over just enough boiling water to cover them. Combine all the ground spices together in a bowl.

2. Heat the oil in a large, high-sided frying pan over a medium heat. Add the onions and garlic and fry for 4 minutes, then stir in the spice mixture and fry gently until the onions are soft.

3. Add the butternut squash, carrots and courgette and fry for 3–4 minutes, tossing to coat everything in the spices. Add the apricots and sultanas (and their soaking liquid), honey, chopped tomatoes and bouillon powder. Bring to the boil, then reduce the heat and simmer for 15–20 minutes, or until the carrots are just tender. Add the drained chickpeas and allow to heat through for a few minutes.

4. Cook the quinoa (see page 214) and then stir through the toasted almonds and chopped coriander. Serve the tagine on top of the quinoa, sprinkled generously with more toasted almond flakes and coriander.

A noodle dish like this is all about textures: silky rice noodles and tofu, tender vegetables with a little bite and the crunch of beansprouts and peanuts, all combined with aromatic herbs and a sweet and spicy sauce. It makes a delicious dinner but I often use any leftovers as a great lunchbox filler the following day.

Lemongrass and Ginger Nutty Tofu Noodles

1. Place the tofu in a bowl with the garlic, lemongrass, chilli and ginger. Cover and marinate in the fridge for at least 30 minutes.

2. Soak the noodles in a bowl of boiling water for 6 minutes (or according to the packet instructions). Drain and set aside.

3. Heat the oil in a wok over a high heat and swirl to coat the sides. Add the celery, carrot, red pepper and spring onions. Stir-fry for 5 minutes until softened. Remove from the pan with a slotted spoon and set aside on a plate.

4. Return the wok to the heat with an extra drizzle of oil if required. Fry the marinated tofu until golden on all sides. Return the vegetables to the pan and toss through with the curry powder, sugar and vegetable stock. Simmer for 5–6 minutes until the liquid has reduced slightly.

5. Add the noodles, beansprouts and herbs. Toss everything together until it's well combined. Serve scattered with handfuls of chopped peanuts and herbs.

Serves 4

350g firm tofu, cut into bite-sized pieces
3 garlic cloves, very finely chopped
2 lemongrass stalks, finely chopped
1 red chilli, deseeded and finely chopped
Thumb-sized piece of fresh ginger, peeled and grated
100g flat rice noodles
1 tbsp sunflower oil
2 celery sticks, finely sliced
1 carrot, peeled into julienne strips
1 red pepper, deseeded and finely sliced
4 spring onions, cut into 3cm batons
1 tbsp curry powder
1 tbsp caster sugar
100ml vegetable stock
Large handful of beansprouts
Small handful each of mint, basil and coriander leaves, plus extra to garnish
Large handful of peanuts, roughly chopped

Most people have come across the mighty Pad Thai but its lesser-known cousin, the humorously titled Pad Prik, is also certainly worth a look. Essentially a dry curry with green beans and whatever protein you choose, it makes for a simple and quick supper. I've added vitamin-C-rich peppers to the mix – feel free to add whatever vegetables you see fit once you've figured out the basic method. Tofu can be found in most supermarkets but try looking for it in Asian supermarkets, where you should also be able to get your hands on kaffir lime leaves.

Tofu Pad Prik

1. Heat the rapeseed oil in a large wok over a medium-high heat. Add the tofu and fry until it has a golden brown colour on all sides. Remove from the wok with a slotted spoon and drain on kitchen paper; set aside.

2. Add the red curry paste to the wok and fry for 2 minutes until it becomes aromatic. Add the green beans and peppers and fry until the vegetables are tender.

3. Return the tofu to the wok and then pour in the vegetable stock, fish sauce and sugar, if using. Simmer for 5 minutes, until the sauce has reduced slightly.

4. Remove from the heat and add the kaffir lime leaves, stirring to combine. Serve with brown rice and scatter with the torn basil leaves and toasted peanuts.

Serves 4

1 tbsp rapeseed oil
250g firm tofu, cut into 2.5cm squares
4 tbsp Thai red curry paste
200g green beans, trimmed
1 red pepper, deseeded and cut into 2.5cm squares
1 green pepper, deseeded and cut into 2.5cm squares
75ml vegetable stock
1 tbsp fish sauce (nam pla)
½ tsp caster sugar (optional)
6 fresh kaffir lime leaves, finely sliced
250g cooked brown rice, to serve
Large handful of Thai basil leaves, torn
Large handful of peanuts, toasted

Roast Cabbage with Carrot Purée and Fried Halloumi

I'm sure you've been in the situation of having nothing in the house, but dinner is still required to be on the table regardless! A quick rummage in the kitchen more often than not results in some decent bounty. This dish is one I came up with in that exact instance. The vegetables are transformed by roasting and the addition of a vibrant spice and a silky sweet purée makes a surprisingly delicious supper.

Serves 4

1 head of sweetheart cabbage, quartered
500g brussels sprouts, trimmed and halved
1 head of cauliflower, cut into florets
1 red onion, thickly sliced but root left intact
Olive oil, for drizzling
½ tsp cayenne pepper
1 tsp smoked paprika
3 large carrots, diced
1 roasted red pepper (from a jar), drained and roughly chopped
3 tbsp natural yoghurt
1 tsp rapeseed oil
100g halloumi, sliced
Sea salt

1. Preheat the oven to 200°C (180°C fan).

2. Place the cabbage, brussels sprouts, cauliflower and red onion on a large baking tray in a single layer. (Use two baking sheets if necessary; it's fairly essential you don't overcrowd the tray otherwise the vegetables will sweat.) Drizzle with olive oil and sprinkle with cayenne pepper, paprika and sea salt.

3. Place in the oven to roast for about 40 minutes, or until the vegetables are tender and slightly charred.

4. While the vegetables cook, steam the carrots in a metal steamer set over a pan of simmering water until they are tender. Transfer to a food processor along with the roasted red pepper, yoghurt and a sprinkle of sea salt. Blitz until you have a smooth purée.

5. Heat the rapeseed oil in a frying pan over a medium-high heat and fry the halloumi slices until golden.

6. Spread each plate with a dollop of the carrot purée and top with the roasted vegetables and fried halloumi slices. Serve immediately.

Mediterranean Vegetable Tart with Goats' Cheese Cauliflower Crust

This delicious tart uses a cauliflower crust, which is a really wonderful healthy alternative to pastry. The crust can also be used as a gluten-free pizza base.

Serves 4

175g aubergine, cut into bite-sized pieces
1 small courgette, cut into bite-sized pieces
1 red onion, cut into bite-sized pieces
1 red pepper, deseeded and cut into bite-sized pieces
2 tbsp olive oil
Pinch of crushed dried chillies (optional)
Sea salt and freshly ground black pepper

For the goats' cheese cauliflower crust
1 head of cauliflower (about 500g), broken into florets
1 large free-range egg
150g goats' cheese
1 tsp dried oregano
Small handful of basil, roughly chopped, plus extra to garnish

1. Preheat the oven to 200°C (180°C fan).

2. To make the crust, place the cauliflower florets in a food processor. Blitz until you have an extremely fine consistency, almost like fluffed-up couscous. Pile the cauliflower onto a large thin tea towel, wrap up and squeeze out as much liquid as you can muster.

3. Transfer the dry cauliflower to a mixing bowl and add the egg, 100g of the goats' cheese, dried oregano, basil and salt and pepper. Mix well to combine; when it starts to stick together, transfer the mixture to a baking sheet lined with parchment paper. Press it out to form a rough oval about 1cm thick, leaving the edges a little thicker for the crust. Place on the top shelf of the oven and bake for 40–45 minutes, or until golden brown.

4. Put all the prepared vegetables into large, non-stick low-sided roasting tin, making sure you don't overcrowd it. Drizzle over the olive oil, season with salt and pepper and toss to coat.

5. Roast the vegetables on the middle shelf of the oven for about 30 minutes, or until the vegetables are cooked through but haven't yet become slightly scorched around the edges. Remove the tin from the oven and allow to cool slightly.

6. When both the vegetables and crust are cooked, spoon the roasted Mediterranean vegetables over the crust, sprinkle with chilli flakes, if using, and spoon on dollops of the remaining goats' cheese. Bake for 10–15 minutes. Scatter over the remaining basil leaves and serve cut into slices.

These light but zesty cakes can be used in salads, wraps and lunchboxes so it is a good idea to make up two batches as they freeze extremely well. I serve them with a vibrant minty salsa verde, a classic Italian sauce that complements the courgettes and peas. Serve it with a lightly dressed rocket salad and it makes a light lunch or a robust starter.

Mini Quinoa, Pea and Courgette Cakes

1. Preheat the oven to 200°C (180°C fan).

2. Heat the rapeseed oil in a large frying pan over a medium-high heat and fry the garlic and onion for 4–5 minutes, or until softened. Add the courgettes and fry for a further 5 minutes until softened. Just before the courgettes are cooked, add the peas and stir through. Set the cooked vegetables aside to cool completely in a large mixing bowl.

3. In a food processor blitz together the pumpkin seeds and flax seeds until they are finely ground. Add the chickpeas, lemon zest and juice and blitz again until smooth.

4. Transfer the mixture to the cooked vegetables in the bowl, along with the spring onions, cooked quinoa, basil and mint. Season with salt and pepper and mix until all the ingredients are evenly combined. If the mixture looks too dry, loosen with 1–2 tablespoons of cold water.

5. Using your hands form the mixture into golf ball-sized balls and then press into 2cm thick patties. Place on a baking sheet lined with parchment paper and bake for 25 minutes, or until golden brown.

6. Blitz all the ingredients for the salsa verde in a food processor until smooth. Transfer to small individual serving dishes.

7. Dress the rocket with a squeeze of lemon juice, a drizzle of extra-virgin olive oil and some salt and pepper; toss to coat. Serve the mini cakes with the salsa verde and dressed rocket.

Serves 6

1 tbsp rapeseed oil
2 garlic cloves, very finely chopped
1 onion, finely chopped
2 courgettes, coarsely grated
100g frozen peas, defrosted
6 tbsp pumpkin seeds
3 tbsp flax seeds
1 x 400g tin chickpeas, drained and rinsed
Zest and juice of ½ lemon
3 spring onions, finely sliced
200g cooked quinoa (see page 214)
Small handful of basil, chopped
Small handful of mint, chopped
Sea salt and freshly ground black pepper

For the salsa verde
6 tbsp extra-virgin olive oil, plus extra for dressing the salad
2 tbsp red wine vinegar
1 tsp Dijon mustard
2 garlic cloves
3 anchovy fillets
1 tbsp capers, drained and rinsed
Handful of flat-leaf parsley
Large handful of mint leaves
½ tsp salt
½ tsp pepper

To serve
3 large handfuls of rocket leaves
½ lemon

Super Power Chilli with Charred Corn Salsa

Making a meatless chilli con carne is surprisingly simple; replacing beef or pork with grains like lentils and quinoa makes for a deliciously light, yet rich and filling meal. You might be thinking it's not going to fool you or the meat eater in your life, but I promise when you serve it up with a spicy smoky corn salsa and all the other accompaniments, nobody will have any complaints!

Serves 4–6

1 tbsp coconut oil
1 large onion, finely diced
1 carrot, finely diced
1 celery stick, finely diced
Large thumb-sized piece of fresh ginger, peeled and finely chopped
3 garlic cloves, very finely chopped
1 red chilli, finely chopped
1 tbsp coriander seeds, toasted and ground
1 tbsp cumin seeds, toasted and ground
1 tbsp chilli powder
1 tsp smoked paprika
250g quinoa
250g Puy lentils
2 x 400g tins plum tomatoes
1 litre vegetable stock
1 x 400g tin kidney beans, drained and rinsed
Sea salt and freshly ground black pepper

For the smoky corn salsa
2 corn on the cob
1 tsp coconut oil
2 tbsp coriander stalks, finely chopped
1 tsp smoky Tabasco sauce

To serve
Natural yoghurt (optional)
2 ripe avocados, thinly sliced
Large handful of coriander leaves
2 limes, cut into wedges

1. Melt the coconut oil in a large casserole over a medium-high heat. Add the onion, carrot, celery and ginger and fry for 4–5 minutes until just tender. Stir in the garlic, red chilli, coriander and cumin seeds, chilli powder and paprika and fry for a further 2–3 minutes.

2. Add the quinoa, lentils, plum tomatoes and vegetable stock and bring to the boil. Reduce the heat, season with salt and pepper and simmer gently for 45 minutes, or until the grains are tender and cooked through. Keep adding liquid if required until the grains are tender.

3. Add the kidney beans and cook for a further 5 minutes. Taste and adjust the seasoning and cover with a lid until ready to serve.

4. While the chilli is cooking, prepare the corn salsa. Boil the corn in a pan of water for 8–10 minutes, or until tender. Slice the cooked corn kernels off the cobs. Heat a large frying pan over a high heat. Add the coconut oil and fry the corn kernels, without stirring, until slightly charred. Stir through the chopped coriander stalks and Tabasco and season generously with salt and pepper.

5. Serve the chilli in deep bowls, topped with avocado slices, spoonfuls of corn salsa, coriander leaves, lime wedges and a dollop of yoghurt, if using.

Mega Beetroot Burgers

Beetroot are easy enough to grow, and there is a huge selection of varieties and colours to choose from, such as pale pinks, candy-striped and even golden yellow. These vegetarian burgers are a great way of showing them off.

Makes 6 burgers

3 tbsp olive oil
1 red onion, finely chopped
2 garlic cloves, crushed
2 raw beetroot, peeled and grated
1 courgette, grated
2 large carrots, grated
100g porridge oats
1 x 400g tin chickpeas, rinsed and drained
3 tbsp tahini
1 large free-range egg
4 spring onions, finely sliced
3 tbsp chopped coriander
Sea salt and freshly ground black pepper

To serve
Wholewheat sourdough buns, split and toasted
Chickpea Hummus (see page 27)
Avocado slices
Beansprouts
Shredded red cabbage

1. Heat about 1 tablespoon of the oil in a large frying pan over a medium heat. Sauté the onion and garlic for 4–5 minutes or until softened. Add the grated vegetables and cook, stirring, for about 5 minutes until softened, then drain off any liquid.

2. Place the oats, chickpeas, tahini and egg in a food processor and pulse to combine. Transfer the mixture to a bowl, stir through the cooked vegetables, spring onions and coriander, and season generously with salt and pepper.

3. Form the mixture into 6 burgers and chill for about 30 minutes (or up to 24 hours). Heat the remaining oil in a non-stick frying pan over a medium heat and cook the burgers, in batches if necessary, for about 2–3 minutes on each side, until golden.

4. Serve the burgers in toasted sourdough buns with the hummus, avocado, beansprouts and red cabbage.

4 Ways Roast Sweet Potato

Indian

Serves 4

4 large sweet potatoes (approx 500g)

1 tbsp rapeseed oil

150g natural yoghurt

1 tsp curry powder

1 garlic clove, peeled and very finely chopped

1 red chilli, deseeded if you wish and finely sliced diagonally

Large handful of coriander leaves

1. Preheat the oven to 200°C (180°C fan). Place the potatoes on a baking tray and drizzle with the rapeseed oil. Bake in the oven for 45 minutes, or until tender when pierced with a fork.

2. Slice open the baked sweet potatoes to reveal the flesh. Mix the yoghurt with the curry powder and garlic and spoon a generous dollop onto each sweet potato. Sprinkle over the red chilli and roughly tear over some coriander leaves.

Mushroom and Spinach

Serves 4

4 large sweet potatoes (approx 500g)

1½ tbsp rapeseed oil

200g forest mushrooms, sliced or roughly torn

1 garlic clove, very finely chopped

100g spinach leaves

Large handful of parsley, roughly chopped

Sea salt and freshly ground black pepper

1. Preheat the oven to 200°C (180°C fan). Place the potatoes on a baking tray and drizzle with about a tablespoon of rapeseed oil. Bake in the oven for 45 minutes, or until tender when pierced with a fork.

2. Meanwhile, heat the remaining rapeseed oil in a large frying pan over a medium-high heat and fry the mushrooms until just tender. Stir through the garlic, season and continue to fry for a further 1–2 minutes. Add the spinach and stir through until just wilted. Mix through the parsley. Slice open the baked sweet potatoes to reveal the flesh. Top with the mushrooms and spinach.

My one healthy eating saving grace when there is very little in the house is a roast sweet potato. Although not exactly fast food, it's worth the wait!

Mexican

Serves 4

4 large sweet potatoes (approx 500g)

1 tbsp rapeseed oil

8 tbsp natural yoghurt

8 tbsp salsa

1 ripe avocado, thinly sliced

Small handful of tortilla chips (about 50g)

Small handful of coriander leaves

1. Preheat the oven to 200°C (180°C fan). Place the potatoes on a baking tray and drizzle with the rapeseed oil. Bake in the oven for 45 minutes, or until tender when pierced with a fork.

2. Slice open the baked sweet potatoes to reveal the flesh. Top each potato with a dollop of yoghurt, the salsa, sliced avocado, crunched up tortilla chips and coriander leaves.

Superseed and Sprouts

Serves 4

4 large sweet potatoes (approx 500g)

1½ tbsp rapeseed oil

200g kale, leaves torn from the stem

1 garlic clove, finely minced

½ tsp chilli flakes

1 tbsp pumpkin seeds, toasted

Small handful of alfalfa sprouts (approx 50g)

Sea salt and freshly ground black pepper

8 tbsp natural probiotic yoghurt

1. Preheat the oven to 200°C (180°C fan). Place the potatoes on a baking tray and drizzle with about a tablespoon of rapeseed oil. Bake in the oven for 45 minutes, or until tender when pierced with a fork.

2. Meanwhile, heat the remaining rapeseed oil in a large frying pan over a medium–high heat. Add the kale and fry for 3–4 minutes, until wilted and tender. Stir through the garlic and chilli flakes, and season. Slice open the baked sweet potatoes. Top with the kale, a dollop of yoghurt, a sprinkle of pumpkin seeds and some alfalfa sprouts.

Sweet Potato Shepherdless Pie

The many shepherds pies I ate during my childhood have nothing on this vegetarian version, which is packed with nutrient-filled ingredients like spinach, sweet potato and quinoa. Coconut oil is the trendy new health ingredient but, fads aside, I use for its exotic sweet flavour and the silky texture it lends to the sweet potato mash.

Serves 4

1 tbsp coconut oil
1 large onion, finely diced
1 large carrot, finely diced
1 celery stick, finely diced
1 garlic clove, very finely chopped
3 thyme sprigs, leaves picked
500g mushrooms, roughly chopped
75ml red wine
500ml vegetable stock
250g quinoa
2 x 400g tins Puy lentils, drained and rinsed
250g spinach
Sea salt and freshly ground black pepper

For the topping
2 large sweet potatoes, peeled and diced
1 tbsp coconut oil
2 red onions, finely sliced

1. Melt the coconut oil in a large pan over a medium-high heat. Add the onion, carrot, celery, garlic and thyme and cook for 4–5 minutes, or until softened. Add the mushrooms and cook for a further 2–3 minutes. Season with salt and pepper.

2. Pour in the wine, vegetable stock, quinoa and lentils and simmer for 15 minutes until reduced. Stir in the spinach until just wilted. Taste and adjust the seasoning.

3. Meanwhile, prepare the topping. Steam the sweet potato in a metal steamer set over a pan of simmering water until it is tender and can be pierced easily with a fork.

4. Melt half the coconut oil in a frying pan over a medium-high heat and add the red onions. Turn the heat down low, season with salt and pepper and cook gently, strring occasionally until softened and caramelised, about 8–10 minutes. Set aside. Preheat the oven to 200°C (180°C fan).

5. Place the sweet potato in a bowl with the remaining coconut oil and mash until smooth. Season to taste and then stir through the caramelised red onions.

6. Transfer the lentil mixture to an ovenproof baking dish and add the sweet potato mash over the top in dollops and spread out evenly across the pie. Place in the oven and cook for 25 minutes until lightly golden. Serve warm from the oven with a green salad.

An authentic dahl is hard to beat. The balance of spices is important so it's worth checking your store cupboard to see what you have got; store spices in airtight containers away from direct sunlight and try to use within 3 months as they will start to lose their flavour. This dahl would be delicious with a simple piece of steamed fish but I love a bowl of it just on its own.

Spiced Indian Dahl

1. Put the lentils into a heavy-based pan with the ginger, coriander stalks and salt then pour over the coconut milk and 600ml of water. Bring to a gentle simmer and cook for 30 minutes, stirring frequently, adding the tomatoes after 10 minutes.

2. After 30 minutes the lentils will have broken down and will be thick and creamy. Then whisk until the mixture becomes smooth. If it is too thick then you can add a little more water. Leave to simmer gently while you get the spice mixture ready.

3. Heat the oil in a small, heavy-based frying pan. Add the turmeric, cumin, coriander, mustard seeds, red chilli and curry leaves to the hot oil – this is known as tempering, where the hot oil brings out the aroma and flavour of the spices. After 30 seconds to 1 minute the mustard seeds should start popping; at this point stir the tempered spices into the lentils, reserving 1 tablespoon. Be careful as the mixture may spit a little. Whisk until well combined and then stir in the baby spinach, lemon juice and sliced spring onions, reserving a few for the garnish.

4. Ladle the dahl into bowls, then sprinkle over the coriander leaves, reserved tempered spices and spring onions.

Serves 4

300g red lentils
1 tsp grated fresh ginger
Handful of coriander, stalks finely chopped and leaves roughly chopped
1 tsp salt
1 x 400ml tin light coconut milk
1 x 400g tin chopped tomatoes
3 tbsp sunflower oil
1 tsp ground turmeric
½ tsp ground cumin
½ tsp ground coriander
½ tsp mustard seeds
1 red chilli, deseeded and finely chopped
8 curry leaves (ideally fresh, but dried is OK)
100g baby spinach leaves
Juice of 1 lemon
2 spring onions, finely sliced

I regularly make this spicy charred fish as the filling for fish tacos. Combined with a cooling sweet mango salsa and a fresh tasting brown rice salad it becomes a hearty yet fresh dinner. Most of the elements can be prepared in advance but only cook the fish when you are ready to serve.

Spiced Fish with Mango Salsa and Brown Rice Salad

1. Cook the rice for the salad according to the packet instructions (or use leftover rice). Allow to cool. Meanwhile, whisk together the garlic, olive oil and balsamic vinegar in a large bowl. Add the cooled rice, chickpeas, asparagus, parsley and rocket and mix until everything is evenly combined. Season with salt and pepper.

2. Make the mango salsa. Cut the cucumber in half lengthways and use a teaspoon to scoop out and discard the seeds in the middle. Cut the cucumber into dice and add to a bowl with the remaining salsa ingredients (except the coriander). Season with salt and pepper and stir well to combine, adding the coriander just before serving.

3. Combine all the ground spices in a bowl and then use the spice mix to dust the fish fillet.

4. Heat a barbecue or griddle pan to a medium-high heat. When hot, brush the grill or griddle with the oil and cook the fish for 4–5 minutes on each side until cooked through (the flesh should be just opaque). Use a couple of forks to break the fish into large chunks. Serve immediately with the brown rice salad and mango salsa.

Serves 4

1 tbsp smoked paprika
1 tsp garlic powder
1 tsp dried oregano
1 tsp cayenne pepper
1 tsp ground cumin
650g skinless cod fillet
1 tbsp sunflower oil

For the wild rice salad
200g cooked brown basmati ric
1 garlic clove, finely chopped
3 tbsp extra-virgin olive oil
1 tbsp balsamic vinegar
1 x 400g tin chickpeas, drained, rinsed and roughly chopped
6 raw or blanched asparagus spears, finely sliced
Large handful of fresh flat-leaf parsley, chopped
50g rocket leaves, roughly chopped
Sea salt and freshly ground black pepper

For the mango salsa
½ cucumber
2 mangoes, peeled, stoned and chopped
4 spring onions, trimmed and chopped
1 small red chilli, deseeded and chopped
Juice of 1 lime
2 tbsp olive oil
Large handful of coriander leaves, chopped
Sea salt and freshly ground black pepper

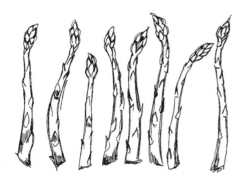

Crispy Spiced Squid with Avocado Salad

This has to be one of the most delicious salads I've ever tasted. It packs a powerful flavour punch that you'll find yourself craving… you have been warned!

Serves 4–6

For the salad

3 firm ripe hass avocados
1 small red onion, finely sliced
150g cherry plum tomatoes, halved
Small handful of fresh coriander, finely chopped
Juice of 2 limes
2 Little Gem lettuces, outer leaves discarded and separated into leaves
Salt and freshly ground black pepper

For the crispy squid

450g medium-sized squid, cleaned
2 tbsp cornflour
3 tbsp semolina
1 tsp smoked paprika
1 tsp sea salt
Sunflower oil for deep-frying
1 red chilli, thinly sliced, to garnish
2 spring onions, thinly sliced, to garnish

1. Cut the avocados in half and remove the stone, then scoop out the flesh and slice thinly. Place in a bowl with the red onion, cherry plum tomatoes, coriander and lime juice. Season with salt and pepper and gently fold everything together.

2. Scatter the Little Gem lettuce leaves over serving plates and then sprinkle over the avocado and tomato mixture. Set aside until needed.

3. Cut the body pouch of each squid open along one side and use a sharp knife to score the inner side into a fine diamond pattern. Then cut each pouch lengthways in half, then across into 5cm pieces. Separate the tentacles into pairs.

4. Put the cornflour, semolina, paprika and a teaspoon of salt into a plastic freezer bag. Add the prepared squid and then toss to coat. Tip out on to a tray, knocking off any excess and leave for 1–2 minutes so that the cornflour mixture becomes slightly damp (this will give a crispier finish).

5. Heat the oil in deep fryer or large pan to 190°C. When the oil is hot enough, which is when it sizzles up fiercely when you place in the top of a wooden spoon, fry the squid in batches for 1–2 minutes. To ensure maximum golden crunchiness don't overcrowd the pan. Drain the squid on kitchen paper and keep warm.

6. Sprinkle the crispy squid over the salad and top with the chilli and spring onions.

This is a great way to jazz up a traditional Sunday roast – here a whole chicken is marinated in yoghurt and spices, making it meltingly tender. The fantastic flavours really penetrate the flesh of the chicken. Try to buy a free-range or organic chicken, as the flavour is always so much better.

Baked Indian-spiced Chicken with Cardamom and Coriander Bulgur Wheat

1. Place all the marinade ingredients into a large non-metallic bowl and mix until well combined.

2. Slash the legs of the chicken several times with a sharp knife – this will give you lovely crispy skin once cooked. Add the chicken to the bowl and rub the marinade all over the chicken, inside and out. Cover with cling film and place in the fridge for at least 4 hours (and up to 24 hours if you have time). Alternatively you can put the chicken and marinade into a large resealable food bag before putting it into the fridge.

3. Remove the chicken from the fridge 30 minutes before you want to put it in the oven. Preheat the oven to 230°C (210°C fan).

4. Arrange the sliced onions over the base of a large oval casserole dish, drizzle with the rapeseed oil and season with salt and pepper. Sit the chicken on top of the onions, which will act as a 'trivet'. Put the lemon halves inside the cavity of the chicken, cover with the lid and place in the oven. Reduce the heat to 200°C (180°C fan) and roast for 40 minutes.

5. Remove the lid and roast for another 20 minutes, basting the chicken after 10 minutes.

6. Meanwhile, prepare the bulgur wheat. Bash the cardamom pods with the back of a knife and place them in a bowl with the bulgur wheat. Add the vegetable bouillon powder and pour over boiling water to just cover. Cover with cling film and leave until all the water has been soaked up and the bulgur wheat is nice and plump, about 8 minutes. Use a fork to fluff up the bulgur wheat and then fold in the coriander and almonds.

7. Let the chicken rest for 10 minutes before carving and serving with the bulgur wheat.

Serves 4

1 x 1.5kg whole chicken
2 large onions, thickly sliced
1 tbsp rapeseed oil
1 lemon, halved
Sea salt and freshly ground black pepper

For the marinade
2 large garlic cloves, crushed
1 tbsp grated fresh ginger
1 tsp ground cumin
2 tsp ground coriander
2 tsp garam masala
1 tsp hot paprika
1 tbsp ground turmeric
2 tbsp rapeseed oil
250ml natural yoghurt
Sea salt and freshly ground black pepper

For the bulgur wheat
3 cardamom pods
200g bulgur wheat
2 tsp vegetable bouillon powder
Handful of fresh coriander leaves, roughly chopped
100g toasted flaked almonds

Pomegranate Molasses Chicken with Roasted Vegetable Bulgur Salad

Roast chicken in any guise tends to grab my attention and this ruby red, glistening one is rather easy to prepare. If you haven't used pomegranate molassses before it is a worthwhile store cupboard ingredient. I use it mainly in beetroot hummus, where it adds both sweet and slightly sour notes, but it is its thick treacle-like consistency that makes it an ideal glaze for meats, particularly chicken.

Serves 4–6

1 large free-range chicken, spatchcocked (ask your butcher to do this for you)
6 tbsp pomegranate molasses, plus extra for brushing
4 garlic cloves
1 red chilli, finely chopped
300g cooked bulgur wheat (see page 214)
Sea salt and freshly ground black pepper

For the roasted vegetables
2 carrots, cut into bite-sized pieces
2 parsnips, cut into bite-sized pieces
2 red onions, root left intact, sliced thinly
3 tbsp olive oil
Sea salt and freshly ground black pepper

1. Place the chicken in a resealable bag with the pomegranate molasses, garlic and chilli. Season with salt and pepper and mix the chicken in the bag so that it's completely coated. Place in the fridge to marinate for at least 2 hours, preferably overnight.

2. When you are ready to cook, preheat the oven to 200°C (180°C fan) and prepare the vegetables. Tip the carrots, parsnips and red onions into a large roasting tray and drizzle with the olive oil. Season with salt and pepper and toss to coat. Make space in the centre of the tray and add the chicken along with the marinade.

3. Roast in the oven for 50 minutes to 1 hour, or until cooked through and the juices run clear when a skewer is inserted into the thickest part of the thigh. The vegetables should also be tender at this stage. About 10 minutes before the end of the cooking time, brush the chicken with pomegranate molasses and return to the oven.

4. Remove the chicken to a chopping board and cover with foil. Add the cooked bulgur wheat to the roasted vegetables in the tray and toss to coat in all the juices.

5. Cut the chicken into breast, thigh, leg and wing portions and place on top of the bulgur wheat. Serve the whole tray straight to the table for your guests to help themselves.

Sticky Sesame and Sriracha Chicken with Chopped Salad

The rise in popularity of sriracha sauce, a spicy hot sauce from South East Asia is hard to avoid. Bottles of this tangy sweet substance are no longer just a staple of Thai street food stalls and can be found in most supermarkets. It can be added to noodles and stir fries for a fiery kick or, as in this sticky chicken dish, with a crunchy salad.

Serves 4

1 tsp rapeseed oil
4–8 skinless chicken thigh fillets, cut in bite-sized pieces
5 tbsp sriracha sauce
Thumb-sized piece of fresh ginger, peeled and very finely chopped
Zest and juice of 1 lime
1 tbsp honey
2 tsp light soy sauce
1 tsp sesame oil
1 tbsp sesame seeds, toasted
Large handful of coriander leaves

For the salad
½ head red cabbage, finely sliced
150g kale, leaves torn from stem and finely sliced
2 carrots, cut into julienne strips
1 tsp sesame oil
1 red pepper, deseeded and cut into bite-sized pieces
1 yellow pepper, deseeded and cut into bite-sized pieces
150g frozen edamame beans, thawed
Handful of cashew nuts, toasted

1. Heat the oil in a wok or a large frying pan over a medium-high heat and fry the chicken pieces until just browned on all sides. Add the sriracha sauce, ginger, lime zest, half the lime juice, honey, soy sauce and sesame oil and toss to coat. Cover and simmer for 8 minutes, or until the sauce has slightly thickened and the chicken is completely cooked through.

2. Meanwhile, prepare the salad. Place the red cabbage, kale and carrots in a large mixing bowl with the remaining lime juice and sesame oil. Massage until the kale becomes tender and then mix through the remaining salad ingredients.

3. Serve the sriracha chicken with the salad and garnish with the sesame seeds and coriander leaves.

This dish is really simple but makes a truly delicious supper – the sweet and exotic flavour of sweet potato and fresh coriander take it to another level. I've used chicken breasts here but chicken thighs are an excellent alternative.

Cajun Chicken with Sweet Potato Smash

1. Start preparing the sweet potato smash. Place the sweet potato in a metal steamer in a pan of simmering water and steam for 10–12 minutes or until just tender. You can add the broccoli for the last 5 minutes of cooking time. Remove the broccoli and keep warm.

2. Transfer the sweet potato to a mixing bowl and use a fork to roughly smash the sweet potato together with the coconut oil and coriander. Season with salt and pepper and keep warm.

3. Butterfly the chicken: place a chicken breast on a chopping board and, with your hand flat on the top of it, use a sharp knife to slice into the thickest part of the breast. Do not slice all the way through. Open out the chicken so it resembles a butterfly and repeat with the other chicken breast.

4. Lay the butterflied chicken on a plate and rub with rapeseed oil. Sprinkle all over with paprika, cayenne pepper, garlic powder, thyme leaves and season with salt and black pepper.

5. Place a large griddle pan over a high heat and cook the chicken for 3–4 minutes on each side, or until cooked all the way through. Serve the chicken with the sweet potato mash and tenderstem broccoli.

Serves 2

200g tenderstem broccoli
2 skinless chicken breasts (about 150g each)
1 tsp rapeseed oil
1 tbsp smoked paprika
1 tsp cayenne pepper
1 tsp garlic powder
3 thyme sprigs, leaves picked
200g tenderstem broccoli
Sea salt and freshly ground black pepper

For the sweet potato smash
2–4 sweet potatoes, peeled and diced
1 tbsp coconut oil
Large handful of coriander, roughly chopped

Warm Duck, Orange, Pomegranate and Mint Salad

The combination of rich duck meat, a salty sharp dressing, the sweet tang and texture of pomegranate seeds and the hit of freshness from the orange, mint and coriander make it particularly special. This is a super winter salad, wonderfully aromatic.

Serves 2

2 duck breasts (about 140g each)
½ tsp sea salt
1 tsp Chinese five-spice powder
1 large orange
4 spring onions, finely sliced
2 large carrots, thinly sliced
½ cucumber, thinly sliced
½ Chinese cabbage, finely shredded
2 large handfuls of salad leaves (baby spinach, baby kale, Little Gem)
Large handful of fresh mint leaves
Large handful of fresh coriander leaves
1 pomegranate, halved

For the dressing
1 tbsp sunflower oil
1 tbsp dark soy sauce
1 tbsp honey
1 tbsp rice wine vinegar
1 tsp sesame oil
Small thumb-sized piece of fresh ginger, peeled and grated

1. Preheat the oven to 200°C (180°C fan).

2. Place the duck on a chopping board and score the skin diagonally with a sharp knife at 1cm intervals. Rub all over with the sea salt and five-spice powder.

3. Place an ovenproof frying pan over a medium heat. Without waiting for the pan to get hot, place the duck in the pan, skin side down, and cook for about 6 minutes, or until the skin is crispy. Tilt the pan towards you and remove the fat with a spoon. Turn the breasts over and then place the pan in the oven for 8 minutes. Transfer to a chopping board, cover with foil and leave to rest.

4. Whisk together all the ingredients for the dressing in a bowl. Using a sharp knife, cut the top and bottom off the orange and carefully slice off the peel and white pith. Cut out the orange segments and set aside. Squeeze any remaining juice into the dressing.

5. Mix together the spring onions, carrots, cucumber, Chinese cabbage, salad leaves and herbs and toss with the dressing.

6. Arrange the dressed salad on a serving plate. Top with orange segments and thin slices of duck. Hold the pomegranate cut side down and bash the skin with a wooden spoon or rolling pin to release the seeds. Scatter over the dish and serve.

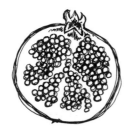

Spiced Lamb Shoulder with Grilled Aubergine and Bulgur Tabbouleh

Lamb shoulder is an often-underrated cut of meat. Slowly cooked and subtly spiced, it's delicious served with a simple yet flavourful tabbouleh and smoky, grilled aubergine.

Serves 4

2 tbsp olive oil
2 tsp ground ginger
2 tsp ground cumin
2 tsp ground coriander
2 tsp ground turmeric
3 garlic cloves
Zest and juice of 2 lemons
Small bunch of coriander
1.5kg lamb shoulder
Natural yoghurt, to serve

For the grilled aubergine
2 aubergines, cut lengthways into 5mm-thick slices
3 tbsp extra-virgin olive oil, plus extra for brushing
1 tsp chilli flakes
Sea salt and freshly ground black pepper

For the tabbouleh
100g bulgur wheat
250ml boiling water
½ cucumber, peeled and diced
150g plum tomatoes, chopped
3 spring onions, finely sliced
Small handful of mint leaves, chopped
Small handful of flat-leaf parsley, chopped
Squeeze of lemon juice

1. Preheat the oven to 160°C (140°C fan).

2. Place the olive oil, ground spices, garlic, zest and juice of 1 lemon, chopped coriander stalks (reserve the leaves for later) and a good pinch of salt into a food processor. Blitz until you have a smooth paste (or use a pestle and mortar).

3. Put the lamb shoulder onto two large pieces of foil and make lots of incisions in the meat with a sharp knife. Rub the paste all over. Add a couple of tablespoons of water, then seal the foil around the lamb, leaving a little pocket of air above it. Place in a shallow roasting tin and cook in the oven for 4 hours.

4. After this time, open the foil and baste the lamb with its juices. Leaving the foil open, cook for a further hour, by which time the lamb should be meltingly tender. Turn off the oven but leave the lamb inside to rest.

5. For the grilled aubergine, brush the slices with olive oil, sprinkle with chilli flakes and season with salt and pepper. Heat a large griddle pan over a high heat and then griddle the aubergine on both sides until they are tender and have visible griddle marks all over. Remove from the pan and keep warm.

6. For the tabbouleh, place the bulgur wheat in a heatproof bowl and pour over the boiling water. Cover with cling film and allow to soak for 10–15 minutes. Drain away any excess liquid and then fluff up with a fork before stirring through the remaining ingredients until well combined. Taste and adjust the seasoning.

7. To serve, carve the lamb into thick slices. Arrange the aubergine on a plate, top with the tabbouleh and slices of lamb and scatter over the reserved coriander leaves.

This salad of simply cooked steak and crisp shaved fennel is dressed with a peppery horseradish sauce. It's not only quick to make but is layered with wonderful fresh flavours, resulting in a winning supper with very little effort.

Rosemary Beef with Horseradish Sauce and Fennel Salad

1. Whisk together the olive oil, garlic and rosemary and brush over the steaks, then season them with salt and pepper.

2. Place a large griddle pan over a medium-high heat and cook the steaks for 2–3 minutes on each side for medium rare (adjust the timings to cook to your liking). Remove from the pan and rest under foil for 5 minutes before slicing into thin strips.

3. Whisk together the ingredients for the dressing in a large bowl. Add the fennel, courgette and red onion and toss to coat.

4. Divide the fennel salad between two plates and top with the rocket leaves, pine nuts and slices of steak.

Serves 2

1 tbsp olive oil
1 garlic clove, finely chopped
1 rosemary sprig, leaves finely chopped
2 small rib-eye steaks
2 fennel bulbs, trimmed and shaved thinly
1 courgette, shaved in rounds
1 small red onion, very thinly sliced
Large handful of rocket leaves per person
75g pine nuts, toasted
Sea salt and freshly ground black pepper

For the dressing
Juice of ½ lemon
1 tbsp natural yoghurt
1 tbsp fresh horseradish, grated
1 tbsp extra-virgin olive oil

4 Ways Side Dishes

Sesame Green Beans

Serves 4

250g green beans, trimmed
3 tbsp tahini
1 tsp dark soy sauce
1 tsp rice vinegar
2 tbsp water
3 spring onions, finely sliced
2 tbsp sesame seeds, toasted

1. Blanch the green beans in a pan of boiling salted water until just tender.

2. In a large mixing bowl, whisk together the tahini, soy sauce, rice vinegar and enough water to loosen the mix until you have a smooth dressing.

3. Transfer the warm green beans to the tahini dressing and toss until completely coated. Serve sprinkled with spring onions and sesame seeds.

Caponata

Serves 4

1½ tbsp olive oil
1 large aubergine, diced into 2cm chunks
1 large onion, finely chopped
2 celery sticks, finely chopped
3 garlic cloves, very finely chopped
1 red pepper, deseeded and cut into 1cm dice
1 yellow pepper, deseeded and cut into 1cm dice
1 x 400g tin plum tomatoes
1 tbsp capers
2 tbsp red wine vinegar
50g pine nuts, toasted
Large handful of basil leaves
Sea salt and freshly ground black pepper

1. Heat 1 tablespoon of the olive oil in a large frying pan over a medium-high heat and fry the aubergine for 10–12 minutes, or until softened. Season to taste. Remove with a slotted spoon and transfer to a plate.

2. Add a little more oil to the pan and fry the onion, celery, garlic and peppers for about 10 minutes, or until softened. Add the tomatoes, capers and red wine vinegar and simmer for 10 minutes, or until the vinegar has evaporated. Season with salt and pepper and stir through the pine nuts and basil leaves. Serve immediately.

During the summer when I cook for friends and family I like the idea that the table has a selection of dishes to choose from, all of which can easily sit on the plate beside grilled meat or fish. These are four great recipes that make wonderful side dishes.

Roasted Cauliflower Doorstops

Serves 4
2 heads of cauliflower
1 onion, thickly sliced but root left intact
1 tbsp olive oil
3 thyme sprigs, leaves picked
Sea salt and freshly ground black pepper

For the lemon, garlic thyme dressing
3 tbsp extra-virgin olive oil
1 garlic clove, finely chopped
3 thyme sprigs
Zest and juice of 1 lemon

1. Preheat the oven to 200°C (180°C fan).

2. Carve the cauliflower into thick slices, about 1cm thick. You should get 3–4 decent slices per head of cauliflower but you can roast the smaller pieces alongside. Lay the cauliflower and onion slices on a large baking tray. Rub all over with olive oil and scatter with thyme leaves and salt and pepper.

3. Roast in the oven for 40 minutes, or until slightly charred around the edges. Whisk together all the ingredients for the dressing.

4. Remove the cauliflower and onion slices from the oven and arrange on a large serving platter. Drizzle with the dressing and serve immediately.

Marinated Courgettes

Serves 4
2 large courgettes, cut into 10cm batons
Table salt
3 tbsp extra-virgin olive oil
3 tbsp white wine vinegar
1 garlic clove, very finely chopped
½ tsp red chilli flakes
1 tbsp dried oregano

1. Place the courgette in a colander and sprinkle all over with salt. Leave to sit over a sink for 1–2 hours to allow any moisture to drain away.

2. Squeeze any remaining liquid from the courgettes and then transfer to bowl. Pour over the olive oil, white wine vinegar, chilli flakes and oregano. Toss to coat, then cover and allow to sit in the fridge for 1–2 hours or overnight.

3. Remove the fridge 30 minutes before serving, to allow the courgettes to come to room temperature.

desserts and sweet treats

I always have room for dessert, even after the biggest meal. It's that change of gear, that icing on the cake, that wonderful end to a delicious meal. While many people eating cleaner diets and lighter food might steer clear of desserts, the recipes here provide some inspirational options that are light, bright, fresh and delicious. Taking into account the many different dietary requirements, this is a collection of some of my favourite desserts, many of which just happen to be gluten-free, sugar-free or dairy-free. Most of them are jam-packed with fresh fruit and – in some cases – a few vegetables have been snuck in there too!

The simplicity of clever cooking at home is demonstrated here with recipes like Fragrant Roasted Rhubarb, scented with ginger and orange and served with cool yoghurt and a sprinkle of vibrant green pistachios, freshly sliced Orange and Pomegranate Salad with Orange Blossom Cream or delightfully simple sharp and sweet Green Apple Sorbet. Lighter bakes also feature, like my moist Carrot and Courgette Cake with Rosemary and Orange Crème Fraîche, the ridiculously addictive and chewy Coconut Macaroons or my rich, dairy-free Peanut Butter Brownies drizzled with dark chocolate.

The desserts here aren't for every day but provide great options for lighter dinner party meals or treats for special occasions. When following a healthy diet it's important to keep a real balance and to still include food that excites you – which is where recipes like these come in!

Fragrant Roasted Rhubarb with Pistachio Nuts

Every year in my garden one of the first plants to make an appearance is rhubarb. The vibrant pink stalks can be used in so many different desserts and even savoury dishes but my favourite way of making them shine is this simple process of slow roasting them until they are tender. The low temperature and cooking time results in rhubarb stalks that hold both their colour and shape. Once cooked they can be enjoyed with granola for breakfast, spooned hot over ice cream or served simply like this with yoghurt, honey and nuts.

Serves 4

500g young or early-forced rhubarb
2 oranges
3 tbsp orange blossom honey
2 whole star anise
Small thumb-sized piece of fresh ginger, peeled and thinly sliced
1 vanilla pod, split lengthways
50g shelled pistachios, roughly chopped
Natural yoghurt, to serve

1. Preheat the oven to 140°C (120°C fan).

2. Trim the rhubarb and then cut across on the diagonal into 5cm pieces. Put into a ceramic baking dish large enough to take all the rhubarb in a single layer snugly. Use a peeler to pare thin strips of orange zest off one of the oranges and add to the rhubarb, then squeeze the juice of both oranges. Drizzle over the honey and orange juice.

3. Add the star anise, ginger and vanilla pod, tucking them in so that they can give the maximum flavour. Cover tightly with foil and roast for 40 minutes.

4. Remove from the oven and allow to cool, leaving the foil in place for 10 minutes.

5. To serve, scatter the roasted rhubarb with the chopped pistachios and put straight on to the table with a bowl of yoghurt so everyone can help themselves.

Orange and Pomegranate Salad with Orange Blossom Cream

This is a mouth-wateringly good dessert, which should be made when citrus fruits are in season and at their best. Feel free to use a mixture of blood oranges, clementines and regular oranges. You can make this several hours in advance, cover with cling film and chill, then just sprinkle with the pistachios before serving.

1. To make the orange blossom cream, whisk the orange flower water into the yoghurt and then fold in the mint, if using. Transfer to a serving dish, cover with cling film and chill until needed.

2. Using a sharp knife, take a slice from the bottom and top of each orange, then place on a chopping board and carefully cut away the skin and pith, following the curve of the orange. Cut the fruit into horizontal slices, reserving any juice in a small bowl.

3. Arrange the orange slices on a large glass plate. Cut the pomegranate in half and, holding the cut side of the pomegranate over the oranges, bash with a rolling pin so that the seeds tumble out.

4. Mix the orange flower water with the reserved orange juice, then drizzle over the top and scatter over the pistachios. Serve with the bowl of orange blossom cream on the side so your guests can help themselves.

Serves 4

4 oranges
1 pomegranate
2 tbsp orange flower water
50g shelled pistachios, roughly chopped

For the orange blossom cream
1 tsp orange flower water
125g coconut yoghurt (such as CoYo)
1 tsp shredded fresh mint (optional)

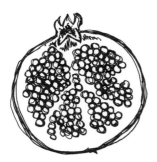

Raspberry and Lime Chia Seed Pudding

This chia seed pudding has to be the ultimate guilt-free dessert; sometimes I even have it for breakfast. I'm a big fan of chia seeds – they have no taste so they take on the flavour of whatever you mix them up with. When soaked in liquid overnight the seeds expand to more than triple their original size.

Serves 4

225g raspberries
200g low-fat coconut milk
250ml almond milk
80g chia seeds
1 tbsp shredded coconut
2–3 tsp clear honey or maple syrup, to taste
Finely grated zest and juice of 1 lime
50g coconut curls, to decorate

1. Put half the raspberries in a large bowl and mash with a fork, then add all the remaining ingredients except the whole raspberries and coconut curls. Stir well to combine. Cover with cling film and chill in the fridge for at least 6 hours, ideally overnight.

2. Divide the pudding into glass serving dishes and top with the remaining raspberries and a few coconut curls.

Green Apple Sorbet

This green apple sorbet is a very clever way to make a sorbet without any of the fuss. It would also work well with frozen mango or peach chunks, mixed summer berries or pretty much any fruit you fancy. Agave syrup or nectar is a natural liquid sweetener from South Africa or Mexico, where it is used to make tequila. It is actually sweeter than honey and has a high fructose content. For a novel way to finish a meal, try pouring a little tequila into the bottom of each serving glass, then scoop the balls of sorbet on top.

Serves 4–6

6 Granny Smith apples, quartered and cored
Juice of 1 large lemon
100–175ml agave syrup
Fresh mint sprigs, to decorate
(optional)

1. Cut the apple quarters in half crossways and toss in a tablespoon of the lemon juice. Arrange on a baking tray and place in the freezer for at least 2 hours or preferably overnight, until completely hard.

2. Remove the frozen apple pieces from the freezer and allow to thaw for 10 minutes before placing in the food processor with the remaining lemon juice and 4 tablespoons of the agave syrup. Whizz until just combined and then pour in just enough of the remaining agave syrup through the feeder tube, to give you a smooth purée that is the consistency of a sorbet.

3. Transfer to a plastic container with a lid and freeze for 3–4 hours, or until firm. This keeps well in the freezer for up to two weeks. Leave in the fridge for 10 minutes before scooping into balls and arranging in small glass serving dishes. Decorate with mint sprigs, if liked, before serving.

Glazed Apple Galettes

A good fruit galette has to be one of the most delicious things to eat. However, it is only as good as its components – choose a fairly tart eating apple, such as new season Cox's or Braeburn and take the time to make the pastry, being careful not to overwork it. I like to serve this with Calvados crème fraîche, which is simply a carton of crème fraîche with a couple of tablespoons of Calvados stirred into it.

Serves 6

3–5 eating apples, peeled, cored and very thinly sliced
30g butter, melted
2–3 tbsp light muscovado sugar
Icing sugar, for dusting (optional)
Calvados crème fraîche, to serve (see above)

For the pastry

250g fine spelt flour, plus extra for dusting
170g butter, diced and well chilled
1 medium free-range egg
1 tbsp balsamic vinegar
1 tsp sea salt
2 tbsp ice-cold water

1. First make the pastry. Place the flour and butter in a bowl and, using a butter knife, cut the butter into the flour until you have a rough pebble mixture.

2. Whisk together the egg with the balsamic vinegar and sea salt. Add this to the butter and flour and using two forks gently toss through until the dough begins to come together. Add a little cold water to bring the dough to a rough ball.

3. Turn the pastry out on to parchment paper or cling film, wrap tightly and chill in the fridge for at least 30 minutes, or overnight is fine.

4. Preheat the oven to 220°C (200°C fan) and line 2 large baking trays with parchment paper.

5. Roll out the pastry on a lightly floured surface until it is about 3mm thick, then cut into 6 evenly sized circles about 14cm in diameter. Arrange them on the lined baking trays. Arrange the apple slices on each pastry circle in an overlapping circle, leaving a 2cm pastry border that is uncovered. Brush lightly with melted butter, then lightly sprinkle with the sugar. Gently fold the pastry border over the apples.

6. Bake the tarts for 15 minutes, or until the pastry is golden and the apples are cooked through. Serve while still warm but not burning hot, dusted with a little icing sugar, if desired. Add a spoonful of the Calvados crème fraîche and be thankful for what you have!

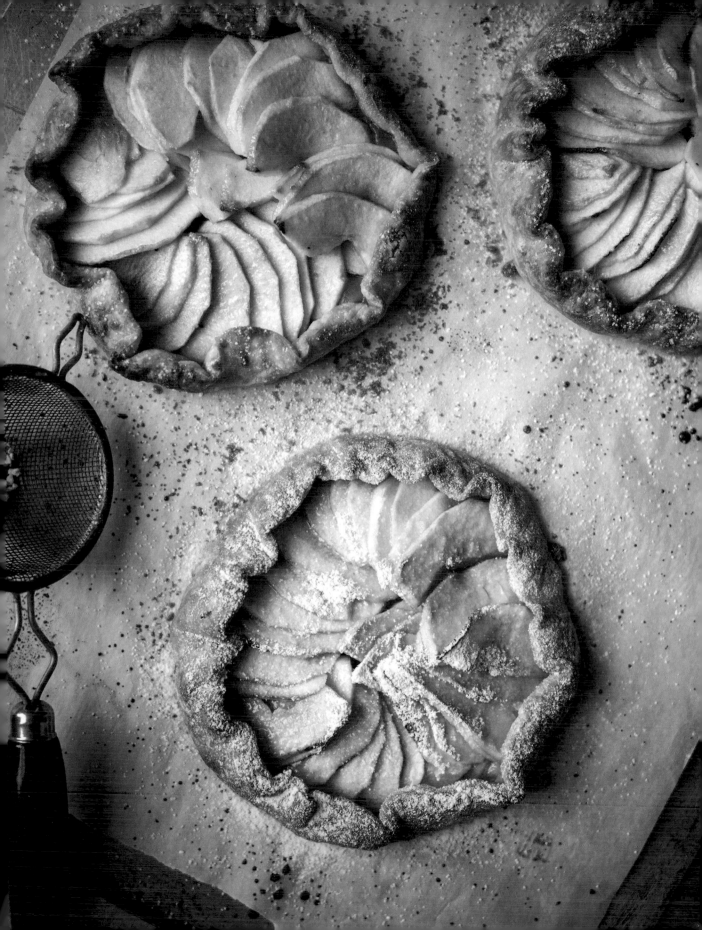

This is a great recipe for a dinner party but you will need to flex your whisking muscles! It's really a fragrant orange jelly topped with a sabayon, which, when made correctly, will be as light as a feather. It is important to whisk it continuously while it cools, to prevent it splitting.

Grown-up Jelly and Custard

1. Using a sharp knife, take a slice from the bottom and top of each orange, then place on a chopping board and carefully cut away the skin and pith, following the curve of the orange. Cut the fruit into segments and arrange in the bottom of 4 Martini glasses. Set aside.

2. Place the gelatine in a bowl of cold water and set aside to soften for 10 minutes. Drain and gently squeeze dry. Place in a small pan with a little drop of the wine and heat gently until dissolved.

3. Warm the remaining wine in a separate pan and stir into the dissolved gelatine mixture. Pass through a fine sieve into a jug. Pour over the orange segments, trying not to disturb the fruit too much. Leave to cool completely and then chill for 3 hours, until softly set.

4. Once the jellies are set, make the sabayon. Place the orange juice in a small pan with the wine and bring to the boil over a high heat. Reduce the heat and continue to simmer for 15–20 minutes, or until the liquid has reduced to about 3 tablespoons. This reduction should be quite thick and syrupy.

5. Place the egg yolks in a heatproof bowl and add the reduced orange juice and wine mixture and sugar. Set over a pan of simmering water, making sure the bottom of the bowl doesn't touch the water, and whisk for 8–10 minutes, until thick and foamy. The sabayon is ready when the mixture is thick and holds its shape when you lift the whisk and let some of the mixture drop back into the bowl. Remove from the heat and sit in a bowl of ice while you continue to whisk until the sabayon has cooled completely.

6. Remove the jellies from the fridge and spoon the cooled sabayon on top. These can be served at once or chilled for up to 24 hours until needed. Decorate with the chopped pistachio nuts and mint leaves just before serving.

Serves 4

2 oranges
6 gelatine leaves
600ml Sauternes or sweet orange Muscat wine

For the sabayon
100ml freshly squeezed orange juice, sieved
300ml Sauternes or sweet orange Muscat wine
3 large free-range egg yolks
2 tbsp golden caster sugar
Chopped shelled pistachio nuts and mint leaves, to decorate

Chocolate Avocado Pudding

A sweet and surprisingly delicious little dessert that will guarantee to have your guests guessing what the secret ingredient is.

Serves 4

3 ripe avocados, stoned and flesh scooped out
75g cocoa powder
1 tsp espresso powder
75g clear honey
3 tbsp coconut milk
1 tsp vanilla extract
½ tsp sea salt, plus extra for sprinkling
1 tbsp raw cacao nibs, plus extra for sprinkling

1. Place the avocados, cocoa powder, espresso powder, honey, coconut milk, vanilla extract, and sea salt in a food processor and blitz until smooth. Stir through the raw cacao nibs until combined.

2. Transfer the mixture to 4 individual serving dishes, cover with cling film and chill in the fridge for 30 minutes until slightly firm.

3. When ready to serve, sprinkle with a little more sea salt and raw cacao nibs.

This crust uses fresh dates, which are available the whole year around, but are at their best between November and January. Fresh dates should be plump and moist with glossy skins. To remove the stones, just push them out with your finger.

Dark Chocolate and Orange Tart

1. For the crust, place the almonds in a food processor and blend for 1 minute, then add the dates, coconut oil, salt and raw cacao powder and continue to blend until well combined.

2. Tip the mixture into a 23cm loose-bottomed fluted tart tin that has been base lined with parchment paper. Use your fingers to spread it evenly across the base and press it into the fluted sides. Cover with cling film and chill for at least 30 minutes while you make the filling.

3. To make the filling, clean out the bowl of the food processor and add the dates with the orange zest and juice, honey, coconut oil and raw cacao powder. Blend together until smooth and then, using a plastic spatula, scrape it into the chilled crust and smooth the top with a palette knife. Chill for at least 2 hours, ideally overnight.

4. To serve, remove from the tin and lightly dust with the cacao powder and grated orange zest before cutting into slices.

Serves 6–8

75g fresh dates, pitted
Finely grated zest and juice of
1 orange
175g orange blossom honey
50g coconut oil, melted
150g raw cacao powder

For the crust
300g blanched almonds
110g fresh dates, pitted
3 tbsp melted coconut oil
Pinch of sea salt
1 tbsp raw cacao powder

To decorate
Raw cacao powder
Finely grated zest of 1 orange

Mocha Chocolate Mousse

Everyone loves chocolate mousse and this one has a wonderful light and airy texture. It is quick and easy to make, and is best served the day after it's made. What's not to love?

Serves 4–6

250g dark chocolate (85% cocoa solids)
6 medium free-range eggs, separated
4 tbsp strong black coffee
4 tbsp almond milk
Chocolate coffee beans, to decorate

1. Melt the chocolate in a large bowl set over a pan of gently simmering water, making sure the bottom of the bowl doesn't touch the water. Remove the bowl from the heat and leave the melted chocolate to cool to room temperature.

2. Once the melted chocolate is at room temperature, whisk in the egg yolks one at a time and then gently fold in the coffee and almond milk.

3. Using a hand-held electric mixer, whisk the egg whites until stiff peaks form, then mix a couple of tablespoons into the chocolate mixture to loosen it. Gently fold in the remainder, using a large metal spoon.

4. Transfer the mousse to individual glasses and smooth the surface. Cover with cling film and chill for at least 2 hours, ideally overnight. Decorate with chocolate coffee beans before serving.

Sticky Toffee Pudding with Roasted Figs

This recipe borrows all the best bits from a traditional sticky toffee pudding but uses figs instead of dates. The result is a dense and rich warm sponge cake, smothered in a slightly alternative caramel and proudly presented with soft, roasted figs. Just try to resist!

Serves 8

175g ready-to-eat dried figs, chopped
1 tsp bicarbonate of soda
160g butter
150g light muscovado sugar
2 large free-range eggs
200g self-raising flour
1 tsp vanilla extract

For the roasted figs
8 firm, ripe fresh figs, sliced in half
2 tbsp clear honey

For the date caramel
75g dates, chopped
4 tbsp coconut oil, melted

1. Preheat the oven to 180°C (160°C fan) and grease and line a 20 x 30cm baking tin with parchment paper.

2. To roast the figs, arrange the fresh figs in a ceramic baking dish, cut side up, and drizzle with the honey. Roast for about 15 minutes until the figs are cooked through but still holding their shape. Remove from the oven and leave to cool at room temperature.

3. Put the dried figs and 300ml water in a pan and place over a medium-high heat. Bring the mixture to the boil and then simmer for approximately 20 minutes or until the liquid has reduced by half and the figs have softened. Use a hand-held stick blender to blitz the mixture until smooth, then stir through the bicarbonate of soda. Set aside.

4. Cream together the butter and sugar in a large bowl with a hand-held electric mixer until light and pale. Add one egg at a time, mixing after each addition, until they are incorporated – if you add the eggs all at once, the mixture can split.

5. Fold the puréed figs, flour and vanilla extract into the pudding mixture until you have a smooth batter. Pour into the prepared baking tin and bake for 20–25 minutes.

6. Meanwhile, prepare the date caramel. Put the chopped dates into a pan with 180ml water and cook gently until softened, about 5 minutes. Transfer to a food processor, add the melted coconut oil and blitz until smooth.

7. Check the cake – it should be risen and firm to the touch and a skewer inserted in the centre should come out clean. Remove from the oven and allow to cool slightly before slicing into 8 generous portions.

8. To serve, spoon some date caramel sauce over each pudding and top with a couple of roasted fig halves.

Lemon and Blueberry Cheesecake

This cheesecake is extra easy because it does not require any gelatine; the action of the lemon juice on the mascarpone and quark helps it set all on its own. The crust uses stem ginger oat biscuits, which can be found in most supermarkets.

Serves 8

Finely grated zest and juice of 4 lemons
200ml clear honey
500g mascarpone cream
400g quark
300g blueberries

For the crust
100g Brazil nuts
100g stem ginger oat biscuits, roughly broken up
150g medjool dates, pitted and chopped
3 tbsp coconut oil, melted
Pinch of sea salt

1. Line a 20cm spring-form cake tin with parchment paper.

2. For the crust, put the Brazil nuts into a food processor with the oat biscuits and blitz until you have fine crumbs. Add the dates, coconut oil and salt and blend again until the mixture is just beginning to stick together. Tip into the prepared cake tin and press it down firmly to create a thin even layer. Chill in the fridge for 30 minutes while you make the filling.

3. For the filling, put the lemon zest and juice and honey into a food processor and blend until well combined. Put the mascarpone and quark into a large bowl and gently fold in the honey and lemon mixture until evenly combined and smooth. Use a palette knife to spread over the crust, then chill in the fridge for at least 4 hours to firm up, ideally overnight.

4. Remove the cheesecake from the tin and transfer to a serving plate. Pile the blueberries on top to serve.

This recipe is based on an absolute classic – the definitive yoghurt cake from a fantastic restaurant in London called Moro. It's delicious served warm or chilled. Orange flower water is now readily available from most large supermarkets or from specialist food stores. It has a beautifully fragrant flavour and is a welcome addition to all sorts of drinks and sorbets. Serve with thick Greek yoghurt with a splash of vanilla extract or the seeds from a vanilla pod stirred through.

Orange Flower, Yoghurt and Pistachio Pudding

1. Preheat the oven to 160°C (140°C fan) and line a 23cm spring-form cake tin with parchment paper.

2. Place the egg yolks in a large bowl with about three-quarters of the sugar and beat until lighter in colour, using a hand-held electric mixer or wooden spoon. Beat in the vanilla seeds, then fold in the spelt flour, orange flower water and lemon zest and juice until well combined. Finally stir in the yoghurt, almond milk and half the pistachio nuts.

3. Whisk the egg whites in a separate large bowl with the remaining sugar until stiff peaks form, using either a hand-held electric mixer (make sure you clean the beaters) or a balloon whisk. Stir one spoonful of the beaten egg whites into the yoghurt mixture to loosen it, then fold in the remaining egg whites, being careful not to knock out too much air.

4. Spoon the mixture into the prepared cake tin and then place in a roasting tray half-filled with boiling water. Bake on the middle shelf of the oven for 20 minutes. Remove from the oven and sprinkle over the remaining pistachio nuts, then increase the heat to 180°C (160°C fan) and return to the oven for another 20 minutes, until the pudding is risen and golden brown. Remove from the oven and leave to cool for about 5 minutes. Don't worry if it drops slightly – that's supposed to happen.

5. Spoon the pudding out on to warmed plates; the base should be like a wet custard with a light sponge on top. Add a dollop of vanilla-spiked Greek yoghurt to each one to serve.

Serves 4

3 large free-range eggs, separated
75g golden caster sugar
2 vanilla pods, split lengthways and seeds scraped out
20g fine spelt flour
2 tbsp orange flower water
Finely grated zest and juice of 1 lemon
300g thick Greek yoghurt
2 tbsp almond milk
40g shelled pistachio nuts, roughly chopped
Vanilla-spiked Greek yoghurt, to serve (see above)

Coconut Cake with Passion Fruit and Mango

All the flavours used for this cake come together brilliantly to create a very more-ish dessert or teatime treat. It looks absolutely stunning and will have your friends begging for the recipe… you have been warned!

Serves 4–6

For the coconut cake
3 large eggs
150g caster sugar
100g dairy-free sunflower spread, at room temperature, plus extra for greasing
100g desiccated coconut
Juice of 1 orange
50g gluten-free flour, plus extra for dusting
1 tbsp gluten-free baking powder

For the passion fruit frosting
100g dairy-free sunflower spread
200g icing sugar, sifted
Generous pinch of sea salt flakes
½ tsp vanilla extract
2–3 passion fruits, halved, pulp scooped out and sieved to remove the seeds

To decorate
1 large firm ripe mango, peeled, and cut into thin slices
1 passion fruit, halved
1 heaped tbsp lightly toasted coconut curls (optional)

1. Preheat the oven to 180°C (160°C fan). Lightly grease a 20cm square non-stick baking tin and then lightly dust with flour or line with parchment paper.

2. Beat the eggs and sugar together in a large bowl with a hand-held electric mixer until light and fluffy. Add the sunflower spread, desiccated coconut and orange juice and beat again until well mixed.

3. Sift the flour and baking powder into another bowl and then fold into the egg mixture, using a large metal spoon. Transfer to the prepared baking tin and bake for about 20 minutes, or until well-risen and golden brown and a thin metal skewer inserted into the centre comes out clean. Leave to cool in the tin for 5 minutes, then transfer to a wire rack to cool completely.

4. Meanwhile make the passion fruit frosting. Place the sunflower spread in a free-standing mixer. Add half the icing sugar and mix for 1–2 minutes to combine. Switch off the machine, scrape down the sides of the bowl with a spatula and add the salt and vanilla extract. Switch back on again, add the rest of the icing sugar and mix until combined. Drizzle in enough of the sieved passion fruit purée to make a nice smooth frosting, scraping down the sides again with the spatula if necessary. Cover with cling film and chill until needed.

5. To serve, spread the passion fruit frosting over the cake with a spatula and then arrange the mango slices on top. Spoon over the passion fruit pulp and scatter with the lightly toasted coconut curls, if using.

Fig, Honey and Almond Cake

Gently spiced and with added texture from the flaked almonds, the cake comes together with a drizzle of sweet floral honey. Do use muscovado sugar if you can, as it is relatively unrefined with much or all of the molasses still remaining, giving it a slightly fudgy, more caramelised flavour. Some cheaper brown sugars are just refined sugar that has been coloured, with none of the authentic flavour.

Serves 6–8

110g butter, plus extra for greasing
150g light muscovado sugar
2 large free-range eggs
210g plain flour, sifted
1 tsp baking powder
Pinch of salt
1 tsp ground cinnamon
2 tsp ground cardamom
12 firm, ripe fresh figs, sliced in half
50g flaked almonds
Floral honey, to drizzle
Vanilla yoghurt, to serve

1. Preheat the oven to 180°C (160°C fan) and grease and line a 20cm spring-form cake tin with parchment paper.

2. Using a hand-held electric mixer, beat the butter and sugar in a large bowl until pale. Add the eggs, one at a time, mixing until they are incorporated. Fold in the flour, baking powder, salt, cinnamon and cardamom until you have a thick cake batter.

3. Finely chop 6 of the figs, leaving the rest cut in halves. Stir through the chopped figs and pour the batter into the prepared cake tin. The batter will be thick, so use a spatula to spread it across the base of the tin. Gently press the fig halves, cut side up, into the batter and sprinkle over the almonds.

4. Bake in the oven for 40–45 minutes, or until a thin metal skewer inserted into the centre comes out clean. Check after 30 minutes and cover the cake with foil if you find the almonds are browning too much.

5. Remove from the oven and leave to cool in the tin. While the cake is still warm, prick it all over with a skewer and drizzle with honey, letting it seep into the holes. Serve generous slices of the cake on plates with a dollop of the vanilla yoghurt.

Carrot, courgette and cardamom are a wonderful combination of flavours. The cake itself is moist enough to serve on its own but for that extra special touch fill and top with this delicious rosemary and orange crème fraîche. This cake will keep in the fridge for 3–5 days.

Carrot and Courgette Cake with Rosemary and Orange Crème Fraîche

1. Preheat the oven to 180°C (160°C fan). Lightly oil two 23cm spring-form cake tins and line the bases with parchment paper.

2. Prepare the rosemary and orange crème fraîche. Pass the orange juice through a sieve into a small pan with the rosemary sprigs and half the caster sugar and simmer until reduced by half. Remove from the heat and allow to cool completely, then remove the rosemary sprigs and discard. Fold into the crème fraîche, then cover and chill until needed.

3. In a large bowl, mix together the flour, bicarbonate of soda, cinnamon and cardamom. In a free-standing mixer (or in a large bowl, using a hand-held electric mixer), whisk together the sugar and eggs until pale and fluffy. With the mixer still on, pour the oil into the bowl in a steady stream and mix until it is completely incorporated, then mix in the vanilla extract.

4. Sift the dry ingredients into the batter and fold in with a spatula until just combined. Add the finely grated carrot and courgette and fold through until completely incorporated. Divide the batter between the two lined cake tins and bake for 30 minutes, or until a thin metal skewer inserted into the centre comes out clean.

5. Remove the cakes from the oven and set aside to cool on a wire rack. When the tins are cool enough to touch, gently release the cakes and return them to the rack, removing the parchment paper. Allow to cool completely.

6. If one of the cakes has risen more than the other, simply trim the excess with a bread knife so that you have a flat surface to work with. Assemble the cake by spreading one of the layers with half the rosemary and orange crème fraîche. Place the second layer on top and spread with the remaining crème fraîche. Decorate with the carrot and rosemary.

Serves 8

275g self-raising flour
½ tsp bicarbonate of soda
1 tsp ground cinnamon
1 tsp cardamom pods, lightly bashed and seeds ground
200g golden caster sugar
4 large free-range eggs
250ml rapeseed oil
1 tbsp vanilla extract
200g carrots, finely grated
200g courgettes, trimmed and finely grated (squeeze out any excess moisture)

For the rosemary and orange crème fraîche
Juice of 2 oranges
2 small fresh rosemary sprigs
2 tbsp golden caster sugar
400ml crème fraîche

To decorate
Carrot strips
Rosemary sprigs

Gluten-free Chocolate Celebration Cake

This cake is good enough to serve at any number of occasions and keeps well in the fridge for several days, as the liquid from the ricotta seeps into the sponge and keeps it lovely and moist. You can make this cake in advance – when it has cooked and cooled, wrap it in cling film and place in the fridge. Then, when you're ready to serve it, allow the cake to come to room temperature before splitting and filling.

Serves 8

4 large free-range eggs, separated
200g golden caster sugar
4 tbsp good-quality cocoa powder, sifted
300g ground almonds
1 tsp bicarbonate of soda, sifted
100ml almond milk

For the filling
500g ricotta cheese
4 tbsp set honey
50g dark chocolate, finely grated (70% cocoa solids)

1. Preheat the oven to 180°C (160°C fan) and line a 23cm spring-form cake tin with parchment paper.

2. Place the egg yolks and sugar in a large bowl and, using a hand-held electric mixer, beat until pale and fluffy. Fold in the cocoa, almonds and bicarbonate of soda. Loosen with the milk until you have a smooth batter.

3. Using a hand-held electric mixer, beat the egg whites until stiff peaks form. Fold the egg whites into the batter, a third at a time, being careful not to knock out too much air. Transfer to the prepared cake tin and smooth down the surface with a palette knife.

4. Bake the cake for about 25–30 minutes, or until the sponge has begun to shrink away from the sides and a thin metal skewer inserted into the centre comes out clean. Remove from the oven and run a round-bladed knife around the edge of the cake. Leave to cool completely in the tin.

5. For the filling, place the ricotta and honey in a food processor and blend until smooth. Fold through half the grated chocolate.

6. Remove the cake from the tin and peel off the parchment paper. Use a serrated bread knife to carefully cut in half horizontally. Spread half of the ricotta and honey mixture over one half and sandwich back together with the other half. Carefully spread the rest of the ricotta and honey mixture on top and scatter over the remaining grated chocolate. Set aside in a cool place until needed.

Fudgy Chocolate Bounty Cake

A deep, dark chocolate cake is the perfect dessert to celebrate with. This one is unique in that it doesn't require flour to bind it but instead relies on ground almonds and some desiccated coconut, which makes it gluten-free but also results in a rich and moist finish. With a glossy chocolate glaze and a topping of toasted desiccated coconut, this cake will be a true showstopper whatever the occasion!

Serves 8

225g dark chocolate, finely chopped
(70% cocoa solids)
125g butter, diced
175g golden caster sugar
1 tsp vanilla extract
100g ground almonds
50g desiccated coconut, plus 4 tbsp
to decorate
6 large eggs, separated

For the chocolate glaze
100g dark chocolate, broken into
squares (70% cocoa solids)
30g butter
50g icing sugar, sifted
4 tbsp cream

1. Preheat the oven to 180°(160°C fan) and line a 20cm spring-form cake tin with parchment paper.

2. For the cake, melt the chocolate and butter in a large heatproof bowl set over a pan of barely simmering water. Remove the bowl from the heat and mix in the sugar, vanilla extract, ground almonds and desiccated coconut with a spatula. Stir through the egg yolks, one at a time, mixing after each addition, until you have a thick batter.

3. Put the egg whites in a free-standing food mixer (or use a hand-held electric mixer) and whisk the egg whites until stiff peaks form. Add the egg whites to the chocolate batter, a third at a time, and fold through gently until just combined.

4. Pour the chocolate batter into the prepared cake tin and bake for about 35 minutes, until it is firm but with a slight wobble. Remove the cake from the oven and sit on a wire rack to cool in its tin. Leave to cool completely before removing from the tin.

5. Melt the chocolate and butter for the chocolate glaze as above. As soon as it is melted, remove from the heat and whisk in the icing sugar and cream. Allow to cool until the mixture becomes thick enough for the whisk to leave a figure of eight trail on the surface. Pour over the chocolate cake and then sprinkle with the desiccated coconut. Leave to set before slicing and serving.

These dairy- and gluten-free muffins are the perfect start to the day with a strong cup of tea. All children love muffins and enjoy getting stuck in when it comes to baking them. Replace the raspberries with blueberries or even dried cranberries for a different result.

Raspberry and Almond Muffins

1. Preheat the oven to 180°C (160°C fan) and line a 12-hole muffin tin with paper cases.

2. Beat the sunflower spread and sugar together in a large bowl until pale and fluffy. Add the eggs one at a time, whisking after each addition until completely combined. Stir through the vanilla extract.

3. Sift in the flour, baking powder and bicarbonate of soda and then fold through, but don't mix too much at this stage. Fold in the ground almonds and almond milk. Finally, gently fold in the raspberries until evenly dispersed.

4. Divide the muffin mixture between the paper cases, filling each one two-thirds full. Bake for 20 minutes, or until golden brown and a thin metal skewer inserted in the centre comes out clean.

5. Leave the muffins to cool slightly in the tin before turning out on to a wire rack to cool completely, then serve topped with raspberries. These are best eaten on the day that they are made.

Makes 12

150g dairy-free sunflower spread, at room temperature
125g golden caster sugar
2 large eggs
1 tsp vanilla extract
150g gluten-free flour
1 tsp gluten-free baking powder
½ tsp bicarbonate of soda
50g ground almonds
100ml almond milk
250g raspberries, plus extra for decoration

Coconut Macaroons

Crunchy on the outside and chewy in the middle, a good coconut macaroon is an irresistible thing. They are also suitable for freezing. To pimp them up, dip or drizzle the baked macaroons with melted dark chocolate.

Makes 16

2 medium free-range egg whites
100g golden icing sugar, sifted
100g ground almonds
Few drops of almond extract
100g desiccated coconut
2 tbsp shredded coconut
50g good-quality dark chocolate, melted

1. Preheat the oven to 150°C (130°C fan). Line 2 baking trays with parchment paper.

2. Using a hand-held electric mixer, whisk the egg whites in a bowl until stiff peaks form. Lightly fold in the icing sugar. Gently stir in the ground almonds, almond extract and desiccated coconut until the mixture forms a sticky dough.

3. Spoon heaped tablespoons of the mixture on to the lined baking trays, and shape into round mounds. Sprinkle a little shredded coconut on top of each one.

4. Bake for 25 minutes: the outer crust should be light golden but the inside needs to be nice and soft. Leave to cool on the baking trays for 1 minute and then transfer to a wire rack and leave to cool completely. Drizzle with dark chocolate and allow to set before eating.

Red Velvet Beetroot Chocolate Cupcakes

Don't be alarmed by the beetroot in these cupcakes; it helps create a rich chocolate batter with just a faint, sweet earthiness. To make a good chocolate frosting, it is really important to beat the butter properly – you'll find that it will go further and taste lighter and fluffier that way!

Makes 12

100g dark chocolate, broken into squares (70% cocoa solids)
200g cooked beetroot
110g golden caster sugar
110g butter, diced, at room temperature
2 large free-range eggs
175g self-raising flour
1 tsp baking powder
50ml milk

For the chocolate frosting
100g butter, diced and chilled
100g golden icing sugar, sifted
1 tsp vanilla extract
2 tbsp boiling water
50g good-quality cocoa powder

1. Preheat the oven to 180°C (160°C fan) and line a 12-hole muffin tin with paper cases.

2. Make the chocolate frosting first: beat the butter in a large bowl until pale and softened using a hand-held electric mixer. Add the icing sugar, vanilla extract and boiling water and whisk again until you have a thick paste. Beat for another minute until the mixture has doubled in volume. Add the cocoa powder a tablespoon at a time, then once it has all been incorporated, beat thoroughly for a final minute. Cover with cling film and chill until needed.

3. For the cupcakes, melt the chocolate in a bowl over a pan of gently simmering water, making sure the bottom of the pan doesn't touch the water. Purée the cooked beetroot until smooth using a hand-held stick blender and then add to the melted chocolate.

4. Beat the sugar and butter together in a large bowl until light and fluffy, using a hand-held electric mixer. Whisk in the eggs, one at a time, until incorporated. Mix in the flour, baking powder and milk and finally fold in the chocolate and beetroot mixture.

5. Spoon the mixture into the paper cases, filling each one about two-thirds full, and bake for 15–20 minutes, or until well risen and firm, and a thin metal skewer inserted into the centre comes out clean. Allow the cupcakes to stand for a minute before transferring to a wire rack to cool.

6. Once the cupcakes are completely cold, spread with the frosting using a small palette knife.

The trick to fluffy cupcakes is to fold the wet and dry ingredients together as briefly as possible – until just combined – and not worry if the mixture still looks a little lumpy. These are best eaten on the day they are made.

Dairy-free Banana and Chocolate Chip Cupcakes with Meringue Frosting

1. Preheat the oven to 200°C (180°C fan) and line a 12-hole muffin tin with paper cases.

2. Mash the bananas in a bowl until smooth, then mix in the vanilla extract. Pour the oil into a jug and beat in the eggs. Sift the flour, bicarbonate of soda and baking powder into a large bowl and stir in the sugar.

3. Pour the oil and egg mixture into the dry ingredients, followed by the mashed vanilla bananas, and stir until only just mixed. Fold in the chocolate chips and spoon into the paper cases, filling each one two-thirds full. Bake for 20 minutes until well risen and golden and a thin metal skewer insrted into the centre comes out clean.

4. Remove the cupcakes from the oven and allow to cool for a minute in the tin and then transfer to a wire rack to cool completely.

5. Meanwhile, make the meringue frosting. Find a pan large enough for the metal bowl of a free-standing mixer to be able to sit in it without touching the bottom of the pan. Pour in 600ml of water and bring to a simmer. Whisk the sugar, egg whites, 2 tablespoons of cold water, lemon juice and vanilla extract in a free-standing mixer until well combined. Transfer the bowl to sit on the pan of water and whisk with a balloon whisk – taking care not to let the mixture boil. Continue to whisk until all the sugar is dissolved (otherwise you'll end up with a grainy frosting). If you have a sugar thermometer it will need to reach 70–75°C.

6. Remove from the pan and return the bowl to the mixer and whisk until nice and glossy and stiff peaks have formed. This will take about 15–20 minutes. Spread or pipe the frosting on to the cooled cupcakes and sprinkle with grated chocolate.

Makes 12

3 very ripe bananas
1 tsp vanilla extract
120ml rapeseed oil
2 large free-range eggs
250g plain flour
½ tsp bicarbonate of soda
1 tsp baking powder
100g golden caster sugar
150g dark chocolate chips

For the meringue frosting
175g sugar
3 large egg whites
2 tbsp cold water
1 tsp lemon juice
1½ tsp vanilla extract
Grated chocolate, to decorate

Susan Jane's Raw Cacoa Nib Fudge

When I first tasted this recipe from my good pal Susan Jane White I was blown away by the flavour – I couldn't believe there was no sugar in it. It really opened my mind to the possibilities of developing dessert recipes that are better for you. Be sure to give it a try and indulge in a true taste sensation.

Makes 25–30 squares

120ml date syrup, plus a little extra if necessary

3 tbsp extra-virgin coconut oil

1 x 340g jar light tahini

Pinch of sea salt flakes

2 tbsp carob powder

2 tsp vanilla extract, plus a little extra if necessary

3 tbsp raw cacao nibs

1. Line a small container, approx 10cm x 10cm, such as a plastic lunchbox, with cling film so that it comes over the sides.

2. Melt the date syrup and coconut oil together in a pan over a low heat. Add all the remaining ingredients, mashing together with a fork and making sure the oil is well mixed in. Taste and adjust with a little more vanilla or date syrup. Work quickly, as the oil will begin to separate from the other ingredients as soon as it starts cooling (it needs a warm environment).

3. Pour your gorgeous, gooey gloss into the lined container. Transfer to the freezer for 4 hours before turning out and cutting into squares. Store any leftover fudge in the freezer, as it will melt quite quickly at room temperature.

Crackerjacks

There are certain tastes that instantly transport you back to being a kid. My aunt Erica used to bring us trays of flapjacks when she looked after us and I've loved them ever since. Here I've added desiccated coconut and sunflower seeds to make them even better for you. This is a great store cupboard recipe that uses ingredients you are bound to have in the house. If you want to make them dairy-free, simply replace the butter with dairy-free sunflower spread or extra-virgin coconut oil. These will store well for up to 1 week in an airtight container.

1. Preheat the oven to 180°C (160°C fan). Grease a shallow 18cm square baking tin and line with parchment paper.

2. Put the rolled oats in a large bowl with the desiccated coconut and sunflower seeds.

3. Melt the butter, sugar and maple syrup in a pan over a low heat until the sugar has dissolved, then pour it into the rolled oat mixture. Mix well, then pour the mixture into the prepared tin and press down well.

4. Bake in the oven for about 20 minutes, or until golden brown. Allow to cool slightly in the tin, then mark into fingers with a sharp knife and loosen round the edges.

5. When firm, remove from the tin and leave to cool on a wire rack. Break into fingers before serving.

Makes 8–10

100g rolled oats
50g desiccated coconut
25g sunflower seeds
75g butter, plus extra for greasing
50g light muscovado sugar
3 tbsp maple syrup

Peanut Butter Brownies with Chocolate Drizzle

This brownie recipe combines two of my favourite things – peanut butter and brownies: together they make the most irresistible treats. Just be careful not to overcook them – the brownie should have a crust, while the middle should still seem slightly moist. You'll be welcome at anyone's house with these!

Makes 24

225g crunchy peanut butter
225g dark chocolate, broken into squares (70% cocoa solids)
150g light muscovado sugar
3 large eggs, beaten
1 tsp vanilla extract
4 tbsp almond milk
100g plain flour
1 tsp baking powder

For the chocolate drizzle
100g dark chocolate, broken into squares

1. Preheat oven to 180°C (160°C fan) and line a 20 x 18cm baking tin with parchment paper.

2. Place the peanut butter and chocolate in a heatproof bowl set over a pan of barely simmering water, making sure the bottom of the pan doesn't touch the water. Stir constantly until melted and smooth.

3. With a hand-held electric mixer, whisk the sugar and eggs together for 2–3 minutes, until pale and fluffy. Slowly add the melted chocolate and peanut butter, then add the vanilla extract and almond milk and continue to whisk until thickened.

4. Sift the flour and baking powder into a separate bowl and then gently fold into the egg mixture. Using a spatula, turn the mixture into the prepared tin and bake on the middle shelf of the oven for 15–20 minutes, or until the top is firm and the brownie has come away slightly from the sides of the tin.

5. Once the brownie is cooked, remove from the oven and allow to cool slightly before transferring to a wire rack to cool completely. While the brownie is cooling, melt the chocolate for the drizzle in a heatproof bowl set over a pan of simmering water. Drizzle the melted chocolate over the top and allow to set before slicing into individual brownies.

store
cupboard

When you scrve up delicious food, making time for those extra touches and elements is what really sets good home cooking apart. Deep and heady spice mixtures that can be sprinkled over eggs, salads or grilled meat and fish; nutritious bread and tasty crispbread; simple sauces dolloped on cooked meat and fish; crunchy caramelised vegetables and pulses that can be added to all sorts of dishes – all these add an extra wow factor and are worth considering when planning your meals.

Roast spiced chickpeas cooked until they are crunchy are a great addition to salads, super seed bread toasted until crisp and homemade crispbread make the perfect vessels for hummus or guacamole, while Middle Eastern spice mixes like za'atar and dukkah add a real depth of flavour to any dish they are added to. You'll also find some delicious dressings and spiced yoghurts, perfect for adding a bit of zing to your salads.

Pistachio Dukkah

Sprinkled on salads or served with bread and olive oil, this dukkah is a taste of North Africa and the Middle East.

Makes 1 small jar

3 tbsp coriander seeds
1 tbsp cumin seeds
1 tbsp fennel seeds
75g pistachio nuts, shelled
50g sesame seeds
1 tbsp sea salt

1. Toast the coriander, cumin and fennel seeds in a dry frying pan over a medium-high heat, until the seeds become aromatic.

2. Use a pestle and mortar to grind the seeds to a rough powder and set aside.

3. Toast the pistachios and sesame seeds in a dry frying pan until they are golden and then roughly chop and add to the spice mix with the sea salt.

4. Transfer to an airtight container and store for up to a month. Enjoy sprinkled over eggs, in salads, with roasted vegetables or simply as a dip with bread and good-quality extra-virgin olive oil.

Za'atar

This spice blend from Arabic cuisine is highly addictive. I sprinkle it over grilled meat and fish or freshly baked flatbreads brushed with olive oil.

Makes 1 small jar

2 tbsp sesame seeds
4 tsp cumin seeds
4 tsp ground sumac
1 tsp sea salt
Small handful of oregano leaves, chopped

1. Toast the sesame and cumin seeds in a dry frying pan over a medium-high heat for about 2 minutes, until the sesame seeds are golden.

2. Place the toasted seeds in a pestle and mortar with the sumac, sea salt and oregano and pound until you have a fine, fragrant and slightly moist powder.

3. Store in an airtight container for up to a month.

Wild Garlic Pesto

Use this simple pesto in sandwiches and grain salads as well as stirred through pasta. You can also make it with basil, rocket or wild nettles plus a clove of garlic in place of the wild garlic.

Makes about 500ml

200g wild garlic leaves, stems cut off, washed and dried
100g pine nuts
120g Parmesan, grated
350ml extra-virgin olive oil
Sea salt and freshly ground black pepper

1. Place the wild garlic, pine nuts and Parmesan into a food processor and pulse until roughly chopped.

2. With the motor running, add the oil gradually, stopping to scrape down the sides of the bowl if necessary. Keep adding the oil until you have the right consistency (you may need to add more if you prefer a looser pesto). Season with salt and pepper to taste.

3. Transfer to clean jars and top with an extra drizzle of oil to create a seal. The pesto will keep in airtight jars in the fridge for at least a week.

Kale is an incredible superfood packed with vitamins and minerals. That aside, it can be transformed into one of the most addictive snacks I know – spicy kale chips! They are very easy to prepare; if you prefer them less spicy simply replace the spice mixture with a generous sprinkle of sea salt.

Spicy Kale Chips

Serves 2

225g curly kale
1 tbsp olive oil
1 tsp smoked paprika
1 tsp garlic powder
1 tsp cayenne pepper
Small pinch of sea salt

1. Preheat the oven to 200°C (180°C fan).

2. Wash the kale and dry thoroughly, using a salad spinner if you have one. Tear the leaves from the stems and then place the leaves on a large baking tray.

3. Mix the oil and spices together until evenly combined and then drizzle over the leaves. Massage into the kale until the leaves are completely coated.

4. Place the baking tray in the oven and cook for 15–20 minutes, until the kale leaves are crisp. Serve immediately.

4 Ways Salad Dressings

Piri Piri

Makes 1 small jar
2 red chillies, chopped
1 roasted red pepper (from a jar), chopped
1 garlic clove
Juice of 1 lemon
6 tbsp extra-virgin olive oil
Sea salt

1. Blitz all the ingredients in food processor until you have a smooth consistency. If you find it too thick you can add more olive oil or loosen it with some water.

2. Store in the fridge for up to 3–5 days.

Soy Ginger

Makes 1 small jar
2 tbsp sunflower oil
1 tbsp dark soy sauce
2 tsp rice wine vinegar
1 tsp sesame oil
Small thumb-sized piece of fresh ginger, peeled and finely grated
1 garlic clove, finely grated
1 tsp sesame seeds, toasted

1. Place all the ingredients in a jar with a tight-fitting lid and shake to combine.

2. Store in the fridge for up to 3–5 days.

Whatever meal you bring to the table, a bowl of salad served with or after it is a great way of getting extra greens into your diet. These are four of the salad dressings I come back to again and again.

French Mustard

Makes 1 small jar
3 tbsp extra-virgin olive oil
1 tbsp white wine vinegar
1 tsp Dijon mustard
1 garlic clove, finely grated
1 tsp honey
Sea salt and freshly ground black pepper

1. Whisk together the oil, vinegar, mustard, garlic and honey in a bowl. Season to taste with salt and pepper.

2. Store in the fridge for up to 3–5 days.

Thai Herb

Makes 1 small jar
1 tbsp caster sugar
Juice of 1 lime
3 tbsp fish sauce (nam pla)
1 garlic clove, finely grated
1 green chilli, finely chopped
Large handful of coriander leaves, finely chopped

1. Whisk together the caster sugar and lime juice in a bowl until the sugar has dissolved. Whisk in the remaining ingredients and then taste to make sure you have the perfect balance of salty, sweet and sour. This dressing can be loosened with a tablespoon of water if needed.

2. Store in the fridge for up to 3–5 days.

Super Seed Bread

Eating more healthily often means cutting out creature comforts like white bread but I still crave things like toast piled with scrambled eggs or a quick snack of bread with nut butter. This bread is the business – sliced thinly and toasted it's the perfect vehicle for almost any toppings.

Makes 1 loaf

100g pumpkin seeds
75g sunflower seeds
50g sesame seeds
250g rye flour
150g wholemeal flour
7g sachet fast action dried yeast
350ml tepid water
2 tbsp honey
1 tsp sea salt
2 tbsp extra-virgin olive oil

1. Toast the seeds in a large dry frying pan over a medium-high heat, until golden brown. Allow to cool and then tip into a large mixing bowl.

2. Add both flours and the yeast and stir with a wooden spoon to combine. Make a well in the centre of the bowl.

3. Measure the tepid water into a jug and then whisk in the honey, salt and olive oil until dissolved. Pour this into the well of dry ingredients and mix together until you are left with a firm dough. Turn out onto a clean surface and roughly knead for a minute or so. Transfer back to the bowl. Cover with cling film and leave to prove for 1 hour, although the dough won't change dramatically in size in that time.

4. Meanwhile preheat the oven to 200°C (180°C fan) and line a 900g loaf tin with parchment paper.

5. Turn the dough out and shape into a loaf. Place in the lined tin and bake for 40 minutes, or until light brown. Remove from the oven and allow to cool completely in the tin on a wire rack.

Caraway Crispbread

Living with a Swede means our kitchen is never without crispbread, a staple ingredient in most Swedish homes. I've taken to making it myself to save the suitcases filled with crumbled crispbread dreams. Thankfully it's quite easy to make and will keep for months stored in an airtight container. The Swedes use a kruskavel (a rolling pin with large studs) to roll out their crispbread, resulting in small dimples all across the surface but it can also made flat.

Makes about 36 crispbreads

350g coarse rye flour, plus extra for dusting
350g wholegrain flour
2 tbsp caraway seeds
7g sachet fast action dried yeast
500ml tepid water
1 tsp honey
Pinch of fine sea salt

1. Combine the flours, seeds and yeast in a mixing bowl and make a well in the centre with a wooden spoon.

2. Measure the tepid water into a jug and stir through the honey and salt. Pour this mixture into the well in the dry ingredients and, using a wooden spoon, slowly mix until you have a rough dough.

3. Turn the dough out onto a floured surface and knead gently for 3–4 minutes, until it becomes smooth. Form the dough into a smooth ball, return to the bowl and cover with cling film and a damp cloth. Leave in a warm place to rise for about 1 hour, until the dough has risen slightly.

4. Preheat the oven to 220°C (200°C fan). Turn the dough out onto a floured surface and roll into a long thin sausage and then cut out small ping pong-sized balls. Roll each ball out into long shapes about 2mm thick and then transfer to lightly floured baking trays. If you want to create a dimpled surface (see above), you can prick the surface with a fork.

5. Bake for about 10 minutes, turning halfway through the cooking time. Allow the crispbreads to cool on a wire rack before transferring to an airtight container.

Wholewheat Flatbreads

These flatbreads are best enjoyed and eaten as soon as they have finished cooking. Clapping the cooked flatbread releases the steam trapped inside creating a softer, flakier texture.

Makes 4

225g wholewheat flour, plus extra for dusting
1 tsp baking powder
1 tsp fine sea salt
40g butter, diced and chilled
Rapeseed oil, for brushing

1. Sift the flour, baking powder and salt into a bowl, tipping in any bran that gets left in the sieve. Add the butter and rub in with your fingertips until the mixture resembles fine breadcrumbs. Make a well in the centre and stir in 6 tablespoons of water to make a stiff but soft dough.

2. Turn out the dough out on to a lightly floured surface and knead for a few minutes until smooth. Divide the dough into 4 balls, flatten slightly and then roll each one out into rounds no more than 5mm thick. Brush with oil and fold in half, then in half again. Roll back into balls and then roll out into rounds again as above.

3. Heat a large heavy-based frying pan over a medium heat. Working one at a time, brush each flatbread with a little oil on both sides and then add to the hot pan. Cook for 3–4 minutes, turning frequently and brushing with oil each time you do so.

4. Remove the flatbread from the pan, place in your palm and clap your hands together 3–4 times, taking care not to burn yourself. Wrap in a clean tea towel and keep warm while you cook the rest.

Roast Spiced Chickpeas

These are ridiculously addictive to snack on as they are, but they are also great added to salads to give crunch and spice. You won't look at chickpeas in the same way from here on in!

Serves 4

2 x 400g tins chickpeas, rinsed and drained
2 tbsp olive oil
½ tsp cayenne pepper
½ tbsp smoked paprika
1 tsp ground cumin
1 tbsp sea salt

1. Preheat the oven to 200°C (180°C fan).

2. Toss all the ingredients in a bowl until completely coated and then spread the spiced chickpeas out on a large roasting tray in a single layer. Roast in the oven for 35–40 minutes, or until crisp.

3. These are best served still warm from the oven. Alternatively, cook several hours in advance and reheat at the same temperature for 10 minutes.

Sweet Potato Chips

Hands-down one of my favourite snacks. They don't go as crispy as regular home-made baked chips but I love their sweet chewiness. To get them at all crispy you do have to cook them right up until the edge of 'charred' so do keep an eye on them right at the end. The sweet starchiness allows for bold spicing, so do experiment with spices like cayenne pepper, cumin or chilli powder.

Serves 2

3 medium sweet potatoes, sliced into thin chips
1 tbsp rapeseed oil
2 tsp Cajun seasoning or smoked paprika
3 thyme sprigs
Sea salt

1. Preheat the oven to 200°C (180°C fan).

2. Toss the sweet potato chips in a large roasting tin with the rapeseed oil, Cajun seasoning, thyme, and sea salt, making sure they are well coated.

3. Pop the roasting tin in the oven for 35–40 minutes. Toss them half way through the cooking time and keep an eye on them – you want them to be slightly charred at the edges. Serve immediately.

Root Vegetable Mash

I've taken to using coconut oil when I make a root vegetable mash like this one – not because of its rumoured health benefits, but because at its core it has a sweet, exotic flavour that complements the vegetables and helps to create a smooth, velvety consistency when they are mashed. If you have time, slowly caramelise some sliced red onion in a pan over a low heat and then fold them through the mash – heaven!

Serves 4–6

950g total of sweet potatoes, turnips and parsnips, peeled and chopped into 2.5cm pieces
1–2 tbsp coconut oil
Sea salt and freshly ground black pepper

1. Place the vegetables into a large pan and fill with cold water to cover the vegetables. Place over a high heat and bring to the boil. Cook for 15–20 minutes, or until the pieces are tender when pierced with a fork.

2. Drain the veg completely in a colander, then return to the pan. Add the coconut oil, and mash until completely smooth. Season with salt and pepper and serve immediately.

Spiced yoghurts feature a lot in my cooking lately –
I find them a great (and slightly healthier) alternative
to mayonnaise or soured cream. Use to top salads, pulses,
falafel or as a dip for grilled meat or fish. Here are a few
of my favourite flavourings.

Spiced Yoghurts

1. Whisk the yoghurt and your chosen flavourings together in a bowl until well combined.

2. Store in a covered bowl in the fridge until needed.

Serves 4

6 tbsp natural yoghurt (preferably probiotic)

For sriracha yoghurt
2 tsp sriracha sauce
1 garlic clove, very finely chopped

For Indian-spiced yoghurt
1 tbsp hot curry powder
1 tsp ground turmeric

For herby yoghurt
Large handful of mixed fresh herbs (coriander, mint, basil), roughly chopped
1 garlic clove, very finely chopped

Roasted Cherry Tomatoes

I eat these roasted cherry tomatoes like sweets, warm from the oven. If I am ever left with a glut of tomatoes I roast them just like this and store them in a jar with olive oil. They are the perfect addition to salads, sandwiches or to serve with grilled meats.

Serves 2–4

250g cherry tomatoes
2 tbsp olive oil
Sea salt and freshly ground black pepper

1. Preheat the oven to 200°C (180°C fan).

2. Slice the cherry tomatoes in half and place, cut side up, in a roasting tin. Drizzle with the olive oil and season with salt and pepper.

3. Roast in the oven for 30–35 minutes, or until the tomatoes have reduced to half their size and become slightly caramelised.

4 Ways Grains

Quinoa

Serves 2
150g quinoa
350ml vegetable stock or water

1. Place the quinoa in a pan with the vegetable stock or water.

2. Bring to the boil over a medium-high heat and cook for 15 minutes, or until tender but still with some bite. Drain away any excess water before serving.

Bulgur wheat

Serves 2
100g bulgur wheat

1. Place the bulgur wheat in a pan and cover with cold water. Place over a medium-high heat and bring to the boil.

2. Reduce the heat, cover and simmer for 8 minutes, or until tender. Drain before serving.

Grains are a big part of my diet not only because of their nutritional content, but also because they bulk out many great dishes while also being fairly inexpensive. They are easy to cook and store ahead of time so they can be added to salads, served alongside meat and fish.

Puy lentils

Serves 2
150g Puy lentils

1. Rinse the Puy lentils in cold water until the water runs clear and then drain. Place in a pan and cover with cold water to come about 5cm above the level of the lentils.

2. Bring to the boil over a medium-high heat, then reduce the heat and simmer for about 15–20 minutes, or until the lentils are tender but still with a little bite. Drain before serving.

Pearl barley

Serves 2
150g pearl barley

1. Place the pearl barley in a pan and cover with water. Place over a medium-high heat and bring to the boil.

2. Reduce the heat and simmer for 50 minutes, or until the grains are tender. Drain before serving.

Index

First published in Great Britain in 2015
by Hodder & Stoughton
An Hachette UK company

1

Recipes and photography copyright © Donal Skehan 2015

Additional photography: pages 9, 13 and 101 copyright ©
James Byrne; page 4 copyright © Rhianne Jones; pages 10, 11,
14, 44, 70, 146, and 192 copyright © Sofie Larsson

Illustrations copyright © Sarah Leuzzi

A CIP catalogue record for this title is available from
the British Library

Hardback ISBN 978 1 473 62103 9
Ebook ISBN 978 1 473 62104 6

Editor: Sarah Hammond
Copy Editor: Clare Sayer
Designer: Louise Leffler
Photographer: Donal Skehan
Food Stylist: Lizzie Kamenetsky
Props Stylist: Polly Rawlings
Illustrator: Sarah Leuzzi

Typeset in Bembo

Printed and bound in Germany by Mohn Media GmbH

Hodder & Stoughton policy is to use papers that are natural,
renewable and recyclable products and made from wood
grown in sustainable forests. The logging and manufacturing
processes are expected to conform to the environmental
regulations of the country of origin.

Hodder & Stoughton Ltd
Carmelite House
50 Victoria Embankment
London EC4Y 0DZ

www.hodder.co.uk

Acknowledgements

Even after working on five cookbooks I can tell you
that the excitement of producing one still hasn't left me!
I'm incredibly proud of this one and it's particularly close
to my heart. There is a huge amount of work that goes on
behind the scenes and for that I am so thankful to everyone
who has helped make this book what it is. A huge and
heartfelt thank you to:

My editor: Sarah Hammond and all at Hodder & Stoughton.

My agent: Rosemary Scoular and the team at United Agents.

Recipe editor and tester: Orla Broderick and Sarah Watchorn.

TV team: David Hare, Robin Murray and Marc Dillon,
Brian Walsh at RTE and Suzanne Weldon at SPAR Ireland.

Food stylist and assistant, and prop stylist: Lizzie Kamenetzky,
Poppy Mahon and Polly Rawlings

The HomeCooked Team: Sofie Larsson, Joanna Carley
and Max the dog.

Portrait photography: James Byrne.

And of course to my friends, family, and my wife Sofie
who make it all worthwhile.

A special thank you also to James, Craig and baby Joshua who
put up with me writing while we stayed with them in LA.

For more recipes visit:

donalskehan.com
youtube.com/donalskehan

And find me on Twitter, Facebook, Instagram, Pinterest,
and SnapChat: DonalSkehan